George Kahumoku, Jr.

A Hawaiian Life

George Kahumoku, Jr.

Paul Konwiser

Foreword by George Winston

Illustrated by George Kahumoku, Jr.

Kealia Press
Lahaina, Hawai'i

Cover design by David Konwiser and Pete Masterson
Book design by Pete Masterson,
Aeonix Publishing Group, www.aeonix.com
Cover photo by Bruce Forrester
Illustrated by George Kahumoku, Jr.

Library of Congress Catalog Number 00-192250
ISBN 0-9704434-0-4

Published by
Kealia Press
P.O. Box 12804
Lahaina, Maui, HI 96761

Printed in the United States of America

For my parents, my grandparents and my children.

—G.K.

Contents

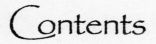

Foreword

George Kahumoku, Jr. is one of the great Hawaiian slack key guitarists, as well as a wonderful composer, songwriter, song interpreter, vocalist, and storyteller. In fact, he is an overall Hawaiian Renaissance Man, also deeply involved in farming, teaching, especially of at-risk teens, and other endeavors.

I began listening to slack key guitar in the early 1970's, a decade when the music was undergoing a heartfelt revival in its native country and a generation of younger musicians were picking up the tradition. It instantly became my favorite tradition and I later founded Dancing Cat Records to record the masters of slack key.

Slack key is the name for the beautiful, solo fingerpicking acoustic guitar style unique to Hawai'i. Each player develops their choice of tunings, techniques, and repertoire, as well as inventing those of their own. The tradition started in the early 1830's, [and predated the steel guitar by about 60 years], as a way to accompany vocals, and evolved into a beautiful instrumental solo guitar tradition as well by the mid 1900's. The Kahumoku family is one of the foremost families of the slack key guitar tradition, having produced three great slack key players so far: George, his brother Moses, and their late father George Kahumoku, Sr.

The biggest inspirations for Hawaiian music and slack key guitar have been the beauty of the islands and the ocean, as well as love for family and friends. There is no better example of this than George Kahumoku, Jr. in his music and the way he lives. These wonderful stories bring the reader into his world.

—*George Winston*

Introduction

The first time I saw George Kahumoku, Jr. perform, I was put under his spell. I think in some ways I've been under that spell ever since. When George takes to the stage, you suddenly find yourself in Hawai'i, sitting in his backyard under a guava tree. His melodies and his voice are a gentle Hawaiian breeze, and you remember how it feels to be there in the islands. And then he draws you in further, with his warm and wonderful stories, so intimate and personal that you become part of his family.

He has always wanted to write some of these stories down, and finally, here they are. If you've had the opportunity to see George in concert, you may have heard some of them, or parts of them. They are highly personal and distinctly Hawaiian. George was raised mostly by grandparents, and in some respects he is like a Hawaiian of a generation or two earlier. But he is also a thoroughly modern fellow who's traveled the world, played music for the Queen of England, and received a mainland college degree. He has even been known to carry around a notebook computer from time to time.

Capturing these stories has been a remarkable experience. George is a fast moving target. Between his full time teaching job at Lahainaluna High School, his farm in Molokai, studio time, his regular music gigs, his road gigs and extensive travel schedule, there's not much time left for interviews. During the past year and a half we have met, among other places, in a swimming pool in Skokie, Illinois, sitting on the grass in front of Lahaina Library, in a scruffy motel in Vienna, Virginia, at a picnic table in Hilo, in front of a bank building in Portland, Oregon, in a barn in Arden, Delaware, under a monkey pod tree on a front porch in Kihei, in my living room at home and in George's house on Maui.

Once you can get him to stop moving, you find that he is in many ways just the man you see on stage. He is also much, much more. He is a kind and generous person, and he is completely forthcoming in talking about his experiences. So much of his day to day life is centered around helping other people. He is, above all, a big hearted man. It has been a wonderful privilege to be able to listen to his stories, and I hope you will enjoy reading them. They are tales of poverty and tough times that illustrate the difficulties of growing up Hawaiian in a modern Western setting. But more than anything, I think, these stories will make you laugh. This is principally because of George's sense of humor, and his ability to overcome life's obstacles with an upbeat attitude and good grace and above all, a very traditional spirit of Aloha.

—*Paul Konwiser*

Acknowledgments

The authors of this book had lots of help and we are grateful. Sandy Miranda willingly volunteered her time, effort and encouragement and made it a much better book. Sandy "Sweetie" Wales spent hour after hour transcribing conversations in pidgin (not her native language), as well as editing and supporting the project. Helen Bigelow patiently edited and critiqued the book from its early stages and is the world's best prufreader (just fooling around, Helen!). Daniel Kuʻuleialoha Palakiko was our Hawaiian language consultant. *Mahalo!* Nancy Sweeney read, commented and provided hugs and hula when we couldn't decide what to write. Colleen Furukawa believed in us and helped us keep moving forward before we had written a word. She also made our pidgin mo' bettah. *Mahalo* also to Patty Kanoholani Delmendo, and Carolyn Nuyen at the Lahaina public library for their help in researching information for the sketches and drawings.

Da Stories

O'O BAR

ALI'I CAPE & KAHILI

Ping! Ping! Thuck!

Now a grandfather myself,
I remember a May morning
Fifty years ago.
A warm day
The air fragrant with plumeria,
On the lanai,
My head on my grandmother's lap
As she gently strokes my hair
And talks story in sweet Hawaiian words,
While in the field behind our house
Grandfather plants taro
Using a long iron stake
Retrieved from a 17th century shipwreck
By his father's, father's, father.
Ping! (He hits a rock)
Ping! (He hits a rock)
Thuck! (Good dirt, and the taro corm is planted).
My grandmother tells me about the *ali'i,*
And how the commoners had to bow to them.
She wanted to be *ali'i*
And bow to no one.

A Hawaiian Life

She knows ancient Hawaiian words, magic words
And claps: One! Two! Three!
And she is *ali'i*.
Others now bow to her.
Ping! Ping! Thuck!
But there are many responsibilities for *ali'i*,
Disputes to settle,
Even decrees of death to make.
And constant travel
On hot rocks
With the sun beating down
The all-powerful sun.
But she can use the magic words
Clap! Clap! Clap!
And she is the sun
Beating down proudly, hotly
On *ali'i* and commoner alike.
Ping! Ping! Thuck!
But too proud, too hot
And the land is scorched and the crops are burnt
And the water dries up
Until the clouds come and cover the land
So the sun does not reach the ground
And is not powerful anymore.
What good to be the sun now?
Magic words!
Clap! Clap! Clap!
And she is the clouds
Raining down powerfully,
So proud, so strong
And the rain fills the rivers and the valleys
And floods the fields where people work

To get their food from the land.
Ping! Ping! Thuck!
What can stop a cloud?
Who is more powerful?
Only one thing: Mauna Loa!
The cloud cannot get by,
It cannot get over.
Use the words!
Use the magic chant!
Clap! Clap! Clap!
And now, she is Mauna Loa
All powerful, it is true
But only rock, immovable
Without thought, without feeling, without soul.
And there on her rocky flanks, a man
Planting taro with an ancient implement.
Ping! Ping! Thuck!
Feeding himself and his family,
Loving his family, and loved by them
In control of his own destiny, all powerful.
The magic words, a last time
Then forget them forever.
Clap! Clap! Clap!
And back to human form
Where grandmother strokes my head
And grandfather plants the taro
And I drift off to peaceful sleep
On grandmother's lap
On a warm morning in May
Half a century ago
To a rhythm of my childhood.
Ping! Ping! Thuck!

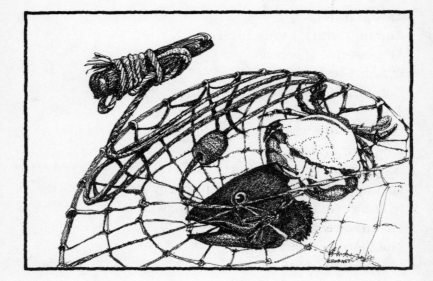

Almost Dead at Six Weeks Old

Some people are really into planning out their lives. They know exactly what they expect to be doing the next day, the next week, the next year. Other people just sort of let life happen and deal with things as they come up. For me, it seems that my life has been a series of accidents, some of them pretty bad things, which have turned out to be blessings in disguise. This pattern started kind of early in my life, at the age of about six weeks.

This was back in 1951. We had moved from the Big Island to Honolulu so my dad could find work. He ended up at the Sewage Department of the City and County of Honolulu. The pay wasn't that good. To help make ends meet, he used to dive for lead in Waikiki. He would salvage the weights from snagged fishing tackle and melt them down into new weights, or into ingots to sell to plumbers for lead piping.

On the weekends, he would borrow this little rowboat and fish for crabs on the Ala Wai canal. Back in those days a lot of people lived on the canal, in pontoon boats floating on 55 gallon drums and smelling of lard and fish and diesel oil. The owner of the rowboat was an old Filipino man named Makatoytoy who lived on one of these pontoon boats. The old man would lend my dad his rowboat, and in return, my dad would patch Makatoytoy's nets.

My dad had been a fisherman in South Kona, so he knew about nets and fishing. In Kona, he used to fish for 'ōpelu — which is Mackerel, ahi — which is yellowfin tuna, and the big Kona crabs. Out in the canal, he had to learn a new way of fishing. He had used much larger nets for the big Kona crabs. In the Ala Wai canal, the crabs were a lot smaller. His crab nets were sort of like basketball rims made of wire, 3 feet in diameter, with the fishing net forming a pocket hanging from the rim. He took *aku* (skipjack) head or *awa* (milkfish) skins and tied them onto a bait string that crossed the round nets. The nets sank to the bottom of the canal and a wooden float marked the location. The crabs would go after the bait, and then get caught in the net when he hauled it back up.

He would make a circuit of the canal for an hour, dropping 30 to 40 nets, then he'd come back to pick them up. Sometimes there would be a dozen crabs in a net, and sometimes it would be empty. He'd put the crabs he caught into a big *pākini,* a galvanized tub, that he kept between his legs as he rowed. He went down and back along the whole length of the canal, all day except for a break when the sun got too hot. He'd sell the crabs at the old Filipino plantation camps in Kahili, or at Palolo housing. That's how he made part of his living. Those were hard times.

My mom was 19. On Saturdays she worked as a car hop at the Capitol Drive-In in Kaimuki, and my dad had to babysit me. I was only about six weeks old when he took me crab fishing for the first time, there in the canal. He put me in the bow of the boat and was rowing backwards. He would row his boat, then he'd throw his nets so you'd hear that sound — shungk — as the net hits the water and goes down.

So he was rowing, picking up nets, throwing them out and wherever he threw out a net, there was a wooden float made out of *hau* wood so he could find the net on the return trip. He'd use a little stick and string that tied the float back to the net. The canal is not very deep, maybe four or five feet, but the bottom is all mud and gook. Originally, Waikiki was swamplands and taro patches. The canal was put in during the depression to collect runoff water from the streams.

He was going along and heard another — shungk — like a net being thrown, but he hadn't thrown anything. He thought to himself, "Oh, must have been a fish jumping." He kept on rowing for a while and then looked around and realized the baby was not there.

He went into a panic, thinking his son has drowned. And then he went into double panic because if he goes home without that baby, he's in big, big trouble with my mom.

He dived into the water looking for his son, but it was so muddy he couldn't see a thing. He searched around for five minutes and could not find the baby.

Ten, fifteen minutes went by and he still couldn't find it. He was frantic. Finally he felt something with his legs, and pulled it out of the water. It was the baby, but it had turned completely blue. It was not breathing and he couldn't even get a heartbeat out of it. So it was with fear and sorrow in his heart that he rushed home bringing this limp blue baby.

He brought the baby to my *tūtū*, my mother's mother, Emily Lihue Ho'opale Dulay. She was a healer. If you had *huli* stomach, she would massage your stomach with olive oil for maybe a couple of hours, and you'd feel much better. She knew a lot about herbs and other things, too.

When my dad brought the baby into the house, she looked at the lifeless body and made a decision: It's not yet time for this baby, he still has a life to live. She knew that the baby's life force had to return so he could fulfill his destiny. And right then and there she gathered together my whole family — aunts, uncles, everybody she could find. They formed a circle placing their hands on the baby.

They started praying on this baby in Hawaiian and my *tūtū* started blowing her breath, her *ha*, all over the baby, blowing and blowing. This was the way it was done then. In old times, Hawaiians didn't kiss. They would hug and rub noses and breathe each other's breath, the *ha*. It is the breath of love and of life.

Finally the baby came alive and that's me. So at six weeks old, I died, and came back to life. Hawaiians have a word, *kūkulu kumuhana*, which means you call on all the powers to be just with you. It's sort of like a laying on of hands, total faith. My *tūtū* believed I had a life.

And a life force entered my body and I was able to live again.

I know about the life force because I've dealt with pigs. There's such a thin line between being alive and being dead. I've seen pigs being born and some of them have a hard time because of problems with the bag they're born in, the placenta. If they don't get that first breath they're dead. I've had pigs where they're born and not taking that first breath and I open their mouth and I blow into the mouth and all of a sudden they come alive and they're just wiggling around. And I've had other pigs that wiggled around but then they lost it. The life force just wasn't in them.

I know how delicate is the veil between life and death. I know it was my destiny to be born and to live. From then on, though, I was very sickly because my lungs had been filled with dirty canal water. I would get colds that went on for weeks at a time. I also had asthma. But that turned out to be a blessing, too. Because by being sickly, I wasn't like the other kids. I got to stay close to my *tūtū*. Everybody else had to go work in the fields picking coffee, or pulling weeds in the coffee and taro patches. I stayed at home.

My *tūtū's* eyesight wasn't too good, but she was used to reading her Bible every night. This was a Bible in the Hawaiian language. So I had to spend all day learning to read in Hawaiian, so I could read to her at night. Like any kid, I wanted to go out and play, but my lessons and all of my chores were indoors. I hated it, but I learned how to read and write.

Whenever I would get discouraged about being cooped up all day, my *tūtū* would tell me, "Your mind is a *huna*, a secret of life. If you can see it in your mind, you can do it. You just have to visualize it. The whole object is to see it in your mind, so dream, dream." She said I could do anything in the world I wanted to do, and I believed her.

As a result of all the reading I did, I got interested in books — all kinds of books, in English as well as Hawaiian. My grandmother would take me to the library. The other kids in my family never got to go to the library, only me.

Eventually I got over the asthma, but by then I had found out about the world outside of the islands, other peoples, other cultures. Each book I read would take me to a whole other place. I knew there was a vast and different world out there. I especially liked some of the old Japanese art books. They taught my mind how to be creative. I discovered that I could draw. We had a horse, Jimmy Boy, that I really loved. I used to draw that horse all the time in my mind's eye. I would draw with charcoal on the ground, or with sticks in the sand, drawing all the things that I saw in my mind.

I went to Fern school in Honolulu for Kindergarten, then Kamehameha School after that. When I was four years old, a drawing of mine won a contest. So I had a scholarship, when I was five, to the Honolulu Academy of Arts. I think that was the beginning. I knew somehow that I was going to be in the arts. You have all of these turning points in your life, and that was definitely one. At eight years old I won another art contest. When I was thirteen I won another scholarship to the Honolulu Academy of Arts. So it went throughout my childhood.

Now in my 50th year, I sometimes look back on my

life and think about how my near drowning changed everything for me. My life was saved by the old Hawaiian rituals and customs of my ancestors. In learning the old ways and the old language, I learned also of the rest of the world. It was the beginning of a long journey that would take me to the Americas, Asia, Europe and Australia. It would eventually lead to a degree in sculpture at a mainland college, and a career as a farmer, teacher and musician. It has made all the difference.

George's bronze and rope sculpture of "Puhi the Eel" can be seen at the Governor's office in Honolulu.

—P.K.

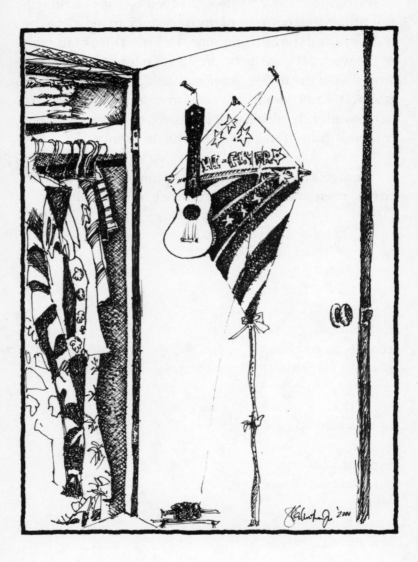

A Stubborn Child

Sometimes I'm asked, "What was the first musical instrument you ever owned?" I guess the short answer is that it was a ukulele. There's a little bit more to the story, though. People who know me well, know that I can be pretty stubborn. I guess to be honest about it, stubbornness is probably a key personality trait for me and always has been. I suppose it might seem kind of funny, now that I am a professional musician, to think that this stubbornness led me to bust up my first ukulele.

When I was about four years old, my brother and I got accepted to Kamehameha Schools in Honolulu. My parents' marriage was kind of on the rocks at that time. My brother Van and I lived with my Auntie Gwendie and my *tūtū* and Grandpa Dulay in a place in Kalihi called Umi Street. With all the Quonset hut houses it was like some kind of wartime tract housing. Their place had a furniture shop in front and a row of houses behind.

Money was a little short in those days. My dad worked for the County, in the sewer department. He used to bring home things he found in the sewers, and put them into bottles and jars he found there as well. We had bottles and gallon jars of marbles, pennies and other stuff lined up against the wall. We didn't have any money for toys then. Mostly I played with string, and I liked to collect interesting rocks and stones. I remember one stone that was my very favorite. I made a holder for it out of string and wore it around my neck for years. It was my lucky stone.

One day Auntie surprised me when she went out to the store taking some of that loose change from the jars and bought me two things. One was this beautiful kite, from the Ben Franklin store. It probably cost a nickel or so. I thought it would look wonderful blowing in the wind. And she also bought me a toy ukulele. In my mind's eye I always thought, "Gee, I want to play like my grandmother." I loved to be with my grandparents there in Kona, watching them play ukuleles and guitars. They wouldn't allow us to touch any of the instruments, because there were so many of us kids, and they knew we would just break them. But now I was going to have an instrument of my own.

So here I had this toy ukulele and I had my kite. I was so happy. But my auntie had what I guess you'd call an ulterior motive for buying me this stuff. She'd use it against me. Like if you don't do this, you don't get to fly the kite or play the ukulele. I grew up with my great grandmother and she never used anything against me like that. If she wanted me to do something she'd just ask and I'd do it. But with my auntie, you had to do this to go get that. She said, "If you are a good boy, you can play with your toys." I didn't even know what the hell a good boy was. I thought I was good.

I must have done something to make my auntie mad. She told me then I couldn't play the ukulele and I couldn't fly the kite. I hung in there for days in anticipation of playing the ukulele or playing with the kite. I didn't know what the heck I had done wrong. I was just a five year old kid. I just got so mad at her. I asked her, "When do I get to fly the kite? Why can't I play with the ukulele?" My *tūtū* in Kona was so different.

To make it worse, Auntie hung the toys on the open closet door, right where I could see them. I saw the kite right there, and the ukulele hanging up next to it and I couldn't touch them. Three, four days went by. To a little kid, it seemed a lot longer. By the fifth day, I was steaming mad about this. She was hanging this thing over my head, like teasing me with a carrot. Finally I couldn't stand it any more.

I went into the closet and took that ukulele and broke it into a million pieces. I took the kite and trashed it, busted it all up. I don't know if it was the spoiled brat in me, but remember, I was brought up by my great grandparents and they treated me like I was *ali'i*, royalty. From my auntie, I got a dirty licking for breaking the toys and I just stood there and wouldn't even cry. She whipped me with her belt and finally she ended up crying instead of me.

I think that's the first time that I realized I had a will of my own and it was really strong, even at four or five years old. And I loved it that I could make my auntie cry. The whippings didn't even hurt me. Maybe a little outside, but I took whatever she dished out and I wouldn't cry for anything.

So that was my first ukulele. It didn't last very long. I guess you could say I started my music career in a pretty strange way, by busting up the first instrument I ever had, even though I was dying to play it. And I saw for myself a strong will that has served me well throughout my life.

The 13 Fight Chicken

Sparing
GLOVES.

Knife

Tape

The 13 Fight Chicken

This is another story about an event in my life that seemed like a bad blow at the time, but that changed my life for the better. I don't know how you feel about cockfighting. Lots of people think it's too bloody and cruel to animals. I'm not making excuses, but for Filipinos and for a lot of Hawaiians, it's simply a part of our culture. I think for farm people, the chance of winning some money with their chickens gave people hope, sort of like the lottery, but with much better odds.

The cockfights were held nearly every Saturday and Sunday in a ranch on the old road just past the theater in Waimanalo. Large amounts of money were being bet on the birds. But these events were much more than a cockfight. Thousands of people turned up every weekend. There were stands selling every kind of local food. They had tables set up where guys played cards and dice and all kinds of other games. Whole families would come, and the atmosphere was kind of like a big dusty carnival or country fair.

Of course, cockfighting was completely illegal in Hawai'i, as it is in nearly every other state. I guess the local cops decided that as a harmless entertainment it could be ignored, or maybe they got paid off by Texeiria, the owner of the ranch. At the cockfights, Texeiria was the law, and as owner of the premises, he got 10% of the winnings. The rumor was that he had killed seven guys with his bare hands. Nobody knew if that was really true, but the reputation was enough to keep everybody relatively honest. There were no problems with thieves, even with all the cash that was changing hands at these events.

When I was growing up, I spent a lot of time with my Filipino grandfather, Grandpa Maning Alagao, who raised fighting chickens to add to a meager income from farming, and from his work as a janitor. On his farm, he had rows and rows of chicken cages. Mostly they were made out of old roofing material and other scrap wood we could scrounge up. At any given time, he'd have about two or three hundred birds.

My grandfather never fought the chickens he raised. What he did was sell them to other people, who took the chickens to fight. My grandfather was well known for his chickens. He'd groom the birds and trim off the comb and he'd practice them for fighting. People would come to the house and look over the birds and select the ones they wanted. Every bird on the farm was for sale, and every chicken cost the same: twenty-five dollars.

But in cockfighting, there is another way a breeder makes money, a thing called *balato*, for good luck. *Balato* means that whoever buys a chicken from a breeder pays the breeder 10% of his winnings on every fight the chicken has. Somebody would buy a bird for $25 and then bet in the thousands when it fought. If the bird won, they gave my grandfather 10% of whatever they won. If they won $2,000 then he got $200. So if he had forty birds that fought that day, he might get $4,000 if half of them won.

I went to the cockfights nearly every weekend with Grandpa Maning. Everybody there knew and respected him. The gamblers also knew me, because for a year or so, I had been working as the bag man for my grandfather. The guys who won with his chickens would come and give the balato to me. I was only 13 years old, but I would often be carrying around thousands of dollars in my pocket. My grandfather trusted me completely. But I couldn't help thinking that whenever one of these guys handed me $100 that meant that he had just made $1,000 with a chicken my grandfather had sold him for $25.

"Grandpa," I asked him, "Why don't we bet some cash on these fights? We could be making choke money."

"Keoki," he told me, "Take a look at these guys. You don't want to be like them do you?"

I had to admit he had a point. The owners of the chickens were, I guess, kind of a shady bunch, some of them. Many of them were professional gamblers.

"Anyway, I bet on the fights sometimes," grandpa said to me. "Twenty five dollars, plenny money to bet. No take big risk."

So that was it for him. He got his $25 and his *balato*. Plus, the owner of the winner got the loser's dead chicken to take home and eat. Back in those days they weren't feeding the chickens chemicals to make them strong.

The owners would usually give the losing chickens to my grandfather, again for good luck. On a good weekend, he would come home from the fights with a half dozen chickens to feed the family. It was enough for him, and he was happy to let others risk their money gambling.

From an early age, I showed some talent for breeding and raising chickens. At a carnival coin toss, I got the coin in the bowl and I won this cute little chick. I was pretty happy about this, so I kept on tossing coins. I ended up with twelve little chicks to take home.

As the chicks grew up they turned into a dozen identical white chickens, with red combs and black wings. Well, almost identical. I could tell them apart. One of them became my favorite pet. I named him Keokea. I could tell Keokea from the others because of a special white mark on the underside of his right wing.

Once they were grown up, of course, they were going to become food for the table, and eventually my chickens' time arrived. We would usually kill several chickens at the same time. My grandfather knew I was attached to this one bird, so the night before he was going to kill the chickens, he said I could keep that special one as a pet. He told me to put him in a separate cage from the others, since he couldn't tell one from another. I was really happy that Keokea was going to be spared.

The next morning, I rushed off to school. It wasn't until I was coming home and telling a friend about Keokea that I remembered that before school I was supposed to separate Keokea from the others. I ran the rest of the way home, and when I got there I found just one chicken in the cage. My grandfather had killed the other eleven.

I opened the cage with my heart in my mouth, hoping it would be my bird. I slowly lifted the right wing, afraid of what I would find. There was no white mark. It wasn't Keokea! That night, the rest of the family enjoyed a tasty chicken dinner. I didn't have any chicken. I was afraid I might be eating Keokea.

Grandpa Maning felt pretty bad about this, so he gave me this chicken that came all the way from Texas. It was a six fight winner that had been blinded one afternoon in a chicken fight. I bred it with a Cuban Red/Black Hatch hen and I kept the chicks. I raised one of the chicks all the way up to a full grown rooster.

It was the only one on the farm that wasn't for sale. This was a beautiful bird. I knew as he was growing up that he was going to be a winner, because of certain characteristics that you learn to spot. His streaks were really dark, black, a sign that he was a good fighter. You looked in his eye, and his pupils were really, really big. The bigger the pupil, the more fierce and brave the chicken is. My chicken was all black, with white streaks running through its feathers. He had black feet and uniform scales all the way down his legs. Just the most beautiful bird you could ever see. He was really attentive. You'd throw him up any way and he'd always land on his feet. Just so sturdy. I worked with him every day for months, tossing him up so he could practice his landing balance and exercising him. I would attach these miniature boxing gloves to his legs instead of knives so that I could spar him with other birds.

After he had his first molt and he was about 18

months old, I told my grandpa that I wanted to fight this chicken.

"OK, Keoki," he told me. "I gave you the bird. He's yours and you can fight him if you want to. But remember, only bet $25."

"But Grampa, this chicken is a winnah. Can make lots of money with him."

I guess my grandfather realized then that it was no use to talk to me. I could hardly wait for the chance to see my special bird do his thing and earn me lots of money.

The following Saturday morning my grandfather and I climbed into his beat-up old pickup truck, and drove to the cockfights. My special bird rode on my lap. Images of my triumphant chicken and a whole lot of cash swirled around in my head. I just knew that this was going to be no ordinary day.

We pulled into the dusty parking lot filled with hundreds of cars and trucks and parked the pickup. We were just climbing out of the truck, when we heard the deep-throated roar of a huge crowd. It was kind of like arriving outside a big football stadium when there's a game already going on and somebody has just scored. This was it, the big leagues.

All of a sudden, I didn't feel so self-assured. I started thinking about the thousands of people there, people not just from Oahu, but from Kauai, Maui and all over. I cradled my bird in my arms, and walked away from the truck, but the confidence was gone from my step. Was my bird really ready? Was he that good? I decided right then that I would only bet $25 on my rooster.

Grandfather and I walked right past the games and

food stands. Usually I got something to eat, but today I was really nervous, and I ignored the wonderful aromas of kalua pig, chicken and rice plate, chili bowls, Filipino plate lunch, adobo, grated coconut with sweetened rice called "bot bot," hot dogs, sodas, all that good stuff.

We walked into the cockfighting arena. People were packed in everywhere, and there was lots of excitement in the air. Cockfights were going on all day long in three separate rings. Two of these rings were called drag pits, where the fights were done on a time limit. If both birds survived five minutes in the ring, it was considered a draw. My bird, in his first fight, would be in the drag pit today. The big ring was for the main event, a fight to the death. As the fights went on, you'd hear huge roars from the crowd, depending on what was going on.

Before the fight, they had to match up the birds. One of Texeiria's guys took my bird in one hand and the other guy's bird in his other hand to compare the weight of the birds holding them up by the legs. There is a kind of handicapping system. The higher the bird is ranked, the higher up they tape the knife on the bird's leg. A one step handicap means the knife is a half inch higher. This gives more leverage and more advantage to a lower ranked chicken.

Meanwhile, there was constant commotion from all these guys hanging around, checking out the competition, arguing with each other, making bets, borrowing money. Another member of the Texeiria gang handled the cash and recorded the bets.

Once the handicap is decided that's it, the money's down and the fight is on. If you're betting on a fight, you have to get your money down quickly or you lose the opportunity. I handed Texeiria's guy my $25.

Finally we were ready to go, and my bird and the other rooster were put down on the ground. I held and stroked my bird, smoothing his feathers and giving him words of encouragement. At the referee's signal, the other bird owner and I let go of our birds and the fight began.

Usually, the birds would kind of size each other up for a moment or two before they really got into it. Not this time. In seconds the other guy's bird was down. My bird just came straight at him and the fight was over.

It was exactly as I had seen it in my mind. I was so excited. I knew my bird and I were unbeatable. I was really sorry I had only bet $25 on my sure winner. I decided that from then on I wasn't going to make any more grandfather-sized bets.

And I certainly was right about my chicken. It was unusual for a chicken to win three fights. A chicken that won a half dozen fights was considered a miracle. And then there was my chicken. He fought every other week for the next six months, and he won 12 fights in a row. And on a sunny Saturday morning in April of 1964, this chicken was going to have his 13th fight.

I had been betting about $100 on each fight. I would have liked to bet more, but my grandfather was giving me some pretty dirty looks. He didn't try to stop me from making these bets. I guess he figured I had to learn about gambling for myself.

I loved and admired my grandpa, but in 12 fights, my chicken had won me a few thousand bucks. I knew grandpa was wrong about gambling and I was determined to make some real money. There were a lot of guys there who had gambling in their blood. You could see it in their eyes. I think grandpa was afraid that I was getting to be one of those guys, and this really bothered him.

When I showed up with my bird that day, I got a lot of attention. Everybody knew this bird and his incredible record, and word spread quickly that my famous 12-fight chicken was going into the main ring. People came over and clapped me on the back and shook my hand. I have to admit, I really was enjoying the celebrity. I was in the thick of things, just this young kid, there in the ring with all these gamblers. I felt right at home.

It took quite some time to match the birds, because of my chicken's record. Because my bird was such a good fighter, he got the knife tied up higher. I had to give the other guy a two step or one inch handicap. I didn't mind. I was completely confident and I knew I couldn't lose. Lots of people had bet on my bird and they were already shouting out for him to win. It really made me proud. Meanwhile, my grandfather's birds had been having an incredible day, and I had all this money on me, probably $10,000. It was obviously our lucky day.

Texiera's guy came over to take my bet. That money was burning a hole in my pocket, burning. I just couldn't stop myself. I handed him the whole wad, bet the whole ten grand on my chicken. The guy looked me in the eye.

"You talk to your grandpa about this?" he asked me. I looked him right back in the eye, but I didn't say anything.

"OK," he said. And he took my money.

A few moments later my brain kicked into gear, and

A HawaiianLife

I thought, "What have I done?" But it was too late, and the guy had disappeared into the throng to start laying off the bet. I just stood there, kind of in shock. I wanted to run away, but the crowd was impatient to begin the fight. I had to settle myself down, focus on my bird. I took extra time with him, holding him carefully, smoothing down the feathers, talking to him. This was one fight he had to win.

Finally we took our chickens into the ring and released them, and the fight was over almost before it began. It went just as it had gone in the other fights, with my bird being the aggressor. My rooster went right after the other chicken and in a couple of seconds the fight was over. A big cheer went up from the crowd, because my chicken was the favorite. I was so happy and excited. I was rich!

The other chicken was on the ground, a goner. He was on his back, his leg with the knife attached, still flailing around. But then my chicken, instead of staying away, kept coming. I guess he wanted to nail the other bird a couple more times. Before I could stop him, my bird put his head right where the other chicken's knife was waving around, and that freaking knife in one swipe, with one last kick, just took the whole damn head off my chicken and it went rolling on the ground.

So both chickens were pretty dead. Normally, that would be a draw. But since the other chicken was still moving around, we had to do something called last peck, or *cadeo*. We hold up the birds to see if one of them would still be able to take a swing at the other. So we held the birds up to each other but mine didn't have a head. The

42

other bird pecked the side of my chicken, so he got the last peck.

The crowd went wild. I had lost all my grandfather's money. When he found out what I had done, he was heartbroken. So was I. In addition to losing the money, somebody else was going take home my chicken and have him for dinner.

That was the last day I was bag man, the last day I was even allowed to go to the chicken fights. It didn't really matter to me, because after that I completely lost any interest in cockfighting and gambling.

At the time it seemed like a major disaster, but as I look back, I realize how my life would have changed if I had won that fight. With a win I would have turned the ten thousand into twenty grand, and I don't think I ever could have stopped. I would have been a gambling addict from then on, just like the shady characters who did this kind of stuff for a living.

Instead, so many other good things happened to me. I finished school, learned about art and farming, and began my music career. Maybe, for me, if not for my rooster, it really was the "lucky 13th" fight. I hate to think that a dumb move by a chicken changed the course of my life, but I have to admit it's probably true.

George Turns Pro

I grew up with a large family on the Big Island. We had a pretty huge front porch and my grandparents would have these parties that would go on for days. We'd have a party to get ready for the party. We'd have a party to get ready for the party that's going to get ready for the party. And eventually do the party. And then have the party after the party.

You had to make sure the people you invited were folks you really liked to spend time with. Hawaiians are very open-hearted. When you had people for your party, there was always the chance that they were going to bring their sleeping bags and camp out for a month in your house. And we're not talking one person, we're talking like a family of 14 or 15. That's how they used to do it in those days.

When we'd get together, all the parents would play music — uncles would play, cousins would play. The jam would go on for days. The kids would sit and watch. Besides me, we had 26 of us little cousins running around like crazy. In our house, we had all these different instruments hanging on the wall — guitars, ukuleles, mandolins, banjos, even a fiddle.

We kids weren't allowed to touch these instruments. If one kid touches, 26 touch and next thing you know, broken instruments. We wanted to get our hands on these instruments and make our own music.

Thinking back on it now, I wonder if our parents were maybe working some kind of reverse psychology on us. I mean, if I'd been forced to take guitar lessons, who knows if I ever would have started playing?

For these big get-togethers, my *tūtū* made something called *'ōkolehao*. What you did in the *imu*, or fire pit, was, you took the ti leaf root and baked it, and the root would come out like black molasses. She'd take that, add water to thin it out, add yeast, and ferment it in a big old bathtub. And way back up in the mountains, she had a little still going and it would drip, drip, drip into this little bottle. She ran the stuff through a tobacco leaf strainer. It would be strained with tobacco and charcoal. I don't know why.

This is how she made her *'ōkolehao*. It was about 200 proof and they called it "green flame." That was their drink. She also bought stuff at the store. Her favorite drink was a thing called Garden Deluxe. It cost something like 79 cents a gallon.

The parents would all get loaded on this stuff and eventually pass out. And when they'd conk out, us kids would grab all the instruments. We'd jump over the stone wall and go into the forest or down to the beach. And that's how we learned how to play. We had guitars, ukulele, mandolins, banjo, everything. Some of them had plenty of strings, some of them had just a few strings. We still managed to learn, by watching the old folks play, and by swiping the instruments whenever we had the chance.

Later, my family was living in Honolulu. This was in the mid 'Sixties, and I was around 13 or 14 years old. I had this beat up old Kay sunburst guitar I used to carry with me everywhere. My mom bought it for me at a garage sale for eight bucks. I had learned to play a little bit of slack key music, just one song really.

I got a job after school and on Saturdays working for Lippy Espinda. He ran a used car lot on the corner of Kalakaua and Kapiolani in Waikiki. Later on, Lippy became kind of famous in Hawai'i for his TV ads for used cars, and he also appeared on a bunch of "Hawai'i Five-O" TV shows. Anyway, Lippy used to pay me to wash cars. I got 10 cents to clean a car, inside and out.

Actually, this was pretty good money for me. I was kind of working under the table, because I was underage. Both my dad and my uncle, Sonny Wailoma, had worked for Lippy before me, so that's how I got the job. I could wash around 10 cars in an evening, so I would make a buck a night. When things were slow, I used to sit in an old rear car seat next to a cinder block wall at the edge of the lot, playing my guitar.

Right next door to the car lot was this sort of a night club. I guess it was more like a strip joint. The name of this place was "The Forbidden City." Several good musicians played there, like Sam Kapu. One of the guys who played regularly was Kui Lee. He went on to become kind of famous, too. He wrote a lot of great songs, like "I'll Remember You" and "It Ain't No Thing."

Kui Lee played there from about five o'clock to maybe nine or ten at night. The musicians took a break at around seven-thirty, and they used to hang around next to the block wall, smoking. On one of his breaks, Kui Lee heard me playing, and he liked it. So he said to me, "Brah, come inside." I knew my folks would kill me if they found out about this. But I went in anyway and played my one song, took me less than three minutes.

And the people in there went crazy, they loved it! They threw money onto the stage. I went outside and counted it up. Several times. Over twenty-seven bucks! I remember because I counted all the loose change. Twenty-seven dollars and ten cents. This was like a whole month's pay at the car wash. So that was the beginning of the end of my car washing career. I knew now that I wanted to become a musician.

A couple of years later, I was playing with four other guys in a band called "The Blue Climax Five." This was in 1966. We won a "battle of the bands" contest at the Waikiki Shell. Well, second place. But by then, we were commanding $35 a night playing in places like the Terrace Club in Kāne'ohe and Alex Rivera's Club Jetty on Kaua'i. I had turned professional.

When I play music, what goes through my head is that I look at the audience like they're part of my family. And when I'm playing, I try to recall different things about the way my family played. On some parts, I think of the way my Uncle Kali used to play the mandolin and tiple. My Uncle Moke would play the guitar and ukulele left–handed, and he had a steady, steady, beat to his music. Then I remember parts my dad used to play, with lots of bass runs. And how my *Tūtū* Koko'o used to sing me songs. Add it all together, it sounds like one person, but I'm actually reminiscing in my mind all the different songs I heard as a young boy listening to the music of my family.

Going for a New Record

Back in October of 1978, I was living in Hilo, on the Big Island. I was still in my drinking days. My brother Moses and I had gone into a recording studio to record the *Hi'i Poi i Ka 'Āina Aloha* (Cherish the Beloved Land) album with Auntie Edith Kanaka'ole. She was close to 70 then, and we were in our 20's. She was such a great composer. While we were in the studio she composed two brand new songs in less than ten minutes. She penned them, she played them, and she said to me, "Look, Keoki — you do this part and I can play that melody." The songs she composed were *He Puna Hele Na Ke Kupuna* and *Napana Kaulana o Keaukaha*, and they were really good.

I was very impressed by this experience, and so was Moses. We had another guy, my younger nephew Ernie Cruz, Jr. with us. He later became famous, playing with a group called the Ka'au Crater Boys, he and Troy Fernandez.

The week after the recording session, over plenty of beers, Ernie, Moses and I decided that if Auntie can create two new songs in ten minutes, three strong young musicians like us should be able to write 200 new songs in two weeks. We gave ourselves a deadline, "This is to-day, in two weeks we're going to create 200 new songs." I borrowed one of those black and white composition books from my *hānai* (foster) daughter, Patty. We figured that would give us incentive to compose. We got started right away, wrote one song, then wrote several others. It seemed pretty easy.

By the time we had gotten to song number 125, we were starting to run out of ideas. So we devised a method for composing. Guy number one would think of a line of lyrics, and then pass the ball to guy number two for the next line. Then guy number three would pick it up. It was a kind of a round robin thing. I guess we were pretty desperate to make our goal. I had a regular job at Alu Like as the director of Native Hawaiian programs during the day, so we had to work on composing on nights and weekends.

By the time we got to song #187, it was 10 days later. We were down at Onekahakaha beach at 2:30 in the morning. We were all feeling pretty good, although not because we were composing so well. I think we were stoned and drunk. We had a couple of cases of baby Millers to help us compose.

We had taken over a picnic table where we could do our work. We had some *pūpūs* (snacks) to eat when we got hungry. They had a little thing like a jukebox that you could put coins in. A quarter turned on the flood-lights for an hour. So we're down there at the beach, with our composition book, our *pūpūs*, beer and a stack of quarters ready to start writing song number 187. It's

Moses' turn to lead off. The wind blows and he says *"Kamakani"* which means "the wind." Then the wind blows again and Ernie Cruz, Jr. says, "Blowing wind." It's now my turn. I'm thinking so hard. I'm trying my best but drawing blanks 'cause it's so late and I'm pretty drunk.

So I pass, like when you're playing cards and you don't have anything, you just pass. The wind blows again. And all we can get out of my brother Moses is *"Kamakani"* again. This time it's Ernie's turn and he can't think of anything so he passes. Now it's my turn and I don't want to pass twice. Our rules were if you pass three times you're out, like when you play cards.

The last word he said was "wind" so I'm racking my brains trying to rhyme to it. I guess because I was a school teacher, my mind goes to the ABC's. So I start with the letter "a," doesn't work. Try b—bin, c—cin, d—din, f—fin, g—gin, no good. When I get all the way to "s" I think of "sk" —skin. So I say, "Touch my skin." And that's how we created song number 187. It goes like this:

Song # 187

Kamakani, blowing wind
Kamakani, touch my skin
Kamakani, you belong
Kamakani, sing my song
You are beauty without a face
And your touch leaves no trace
The sweetness of your breath is here to stay
Kamakani, blow my way.

I often perform this song for audiences and tell the story of how it was written. That's how we wrote a lot of the other songs, too. First we wrote them down in the book, and later on we added the music. We tried to fill up the composition book, doing the lyrics first. Other times we'd play the melody straight to a hand held tape recorder, and just label it "instrumental # whatever."

You know, we did finally make it to song 200. Some people hear this story and song number 187, and they like the song. So then they ask me if I can do some of the other 200 songs. I'd like to, but somewhere over the years I lost that composition book and I don't know where it is. Out of all those 200 songs this is the only one I remember, song #187. So that's the one I always play.

Meanwhile, the two songs Auntie did in the studio that day are still performed today. So since we big, strong, young guys only have one song to show for our efforts, I guess that little old Auntie Edith Kanaka'ole beat us after all.

A Shark Attacks

A Shark Attacks

On a warm, sunny Sunday a couple of days before Christmas, I was out in the sea in an outrigger canoe a mile off the coast of Kona, on the Big Island of Hawai'i. Just a few months before, I was flying high over this same ocean at 600 miles per hour returning from several years of college on the mainland.

During those years, I had felt so separated from my home and culture. But on this day, I would be living the life my ancestors had lived for generation after generation, fishing in the waters around the island. The softly perfumed breeze of the trade winds, and the ocean swells lapping quietly against the boat felt comfortable and familiar. And yet, after years in a big mainland city, it was kind of an adventure, too.

This adventure actually began the day before. I was wrapping up class at the school where I taught. The classroom, on the side of a volcano and surrounded by palm and guava trees, was decorated with the usual Christmas stuff — pictures of sleighs, cardboard snowmen, paper icicles and snowflakes cut out of folded paper. I hoped Santa wouldn't be expecting chimneys here, or we'd be in big trouble.

Late in the day, I saw my 15-year old nephew, Sweetie, hanging around just outside the classroom. He was acting so nervous and sneaky, you couldn't help but notice him. Finally the bell rang, but he waited for the classroom to empty before he came in. It wasn't like Sweetie to be anywhere near school when he didn't have class, and I wondered what was up.

"Aloha, Uncle."

"Eh, Sweetie, howzit?"

He made one final check around the room to make sure we had privacy.

"You still got some *'ōpelu?*"

The *'ōpelu* is a type of mackerel, very tasty. A few weeks before, we'd had a good run on them. I'd saved a few dozen frozen in seawater in milk cartons. Sometimes during the winter months, when *'ōpelu* was scarce, it was handy to have some available for bait. Sweetie was about the only person who knew I had them.

"Yeah, still got some. Why?"

Sweetie took a long, careful look over each shoulder before stepping closer and confiding, "Ahi."

The magic word. When the ahi, the yellowfin tuna, were running, you had a chance to make some real money. I hadn't been paying attention to prices lately, but Sweetie, like me, came from a long line of fishermen and he stayed on top of stuff like this.

"How much they going for?" I whispered. Now I was part of this conspiracy.

Sweetie checked the room again before showing me three extended fingers. He grinned at my surprised reaction. I began to slip from the "textbook" English of a school teacher into my native pidgin.

"Holy shit!" I said. "Tree bucks one pound?"

"Mitchy Alani wen catch one 80 poundah yestahday."

"How you know dis?"

"Arley seen it. He wen see Mitchy bring da canoe in." Arley was Sweetie's little brother. He was only nine years old, but a *very* reliable source of information.

"Somebody else wen see'em?"

"Nah. Jus da same guys down dere. Mitchy said he nevah catch nutting. But Arley tink he acting kinda funny kine, so da buggah stick aroun' when everybody wen go. He wen go climb da coconut tree and go hide on top da tree. Mitchy wen go back to da canoe. He wen take one ahi, put da buggah inside his truck and take off. Arley seen da whole ting."

You don't put anything over on Arley. So the ahi were running, and I had the bait.

"Sweetie, you got some hooks, brah?"

"No, brah."

This was a problem. I knew I had two, maybe three hooks. Hell, if we started buying or worse, borrowing these huge #11 ahi hooks, word would be all over Kealia in hours. Then we'd have 50 other canoes out there trying to catch ahi. It may be the "Big" Island, but it's a small world here when it comes to stories about an ahi run. Sweetie and I decided we'd have to go with whatever we had. We agreed to meet early the next morning at the beach. I'd supply the bait and tackle and outboard motor, and Sweetie would arrange for a canoe.

Just before dawn the next morning, Sweetie and I were driving in my ancient Jeep Wagoneer along the road to a beach near Kealia. We were looking for Arley. Arley was out looking for rocks. He seemed to have gotten lost. I hated driving around like this because my clutch was slipping pretty bad. Parts are expensive in the islands and I was putting off repairs until I had a few extra bucks.

Finally, my headlights picked him up walking along the edge of the road, a skinny kid in well-worn swim shorts, no shirt, no shoes. He was carrying an old white plastic spackle bucket. I saw him bend over to pick up a rock, look it over carefully, and toss it away. No wonder it was taking him so long to collect a bucket of rocks. I pulled the truck up next to him.

"Eh! What you get?" I said, and opened the door for him. He held up the bucket for me to see what was inside, three dozen or so baseball-sized rocks.

"Yeah, dat's 'nuff," I told him. He put the bucket in the back of the truck and climbed in. I put the jeep in gear with a grinding crunch and we headed down to the beach.

"Eh Arley. Dah ahi going fo' three bucks a pound, yeah? So how much fo' one fish weigh 80 pounds?" A question from Mr. Kahumoku, high school teacher. Arley worked the problem in his head, then looked at me in astonishment.

"Dat's 240 bucks!"

Smart kid.

"Fo' one fish?" he asked.

"Fo' one fish."

"Shit! Drive fastah, Uncle."

I laughed, "Gotta catch 'em first." Kids think it's so simple. But it was a chance to pick up, on my one day off, maybe a couple of months' teachers' salary for me, and a year's pay for Sweetie.

We drove on down to the beach, where the canoe was supposed to be. Sweetie's dad, Uncle Poli, was always bragging about his wonderful canoe. But a couple of people had told me to look for a canoe with the ugliest paintjob ever seen on a boat of any size. I laughed at the time, but it was no damn joke. This thing was painted a bright, horrible orange color. It wouldn't have been so bad if the paint hadn't had some kind of ugly fluorescence to it. Poli had painted it a year ago using some marine paint he got on closeout at Sears. No wonder he got it cheap. The *ama*, the outrigger, was all waterlogged and busted up. It was held together with baling wire, old hand line and enough duct tape to keep the Titanic floating.

"Dat's it," Sweetie said.

"What kine canoe dis? Hooo, dat one ugly buggah!" I said. He couldn't really disagree. It kind of took your breath away. We shut down the truck and got out and walked over to the thing.

"You sure da buggah not goin' sink?" I said.

"Nah, Pops says she no leak."

Some people might think it's kind of risky going after large gamefish in deep water with hand lines in a 24 foot boat, even when the equipment is in top condition. With this canoe beneath us, we would really be letting it all hang out.

But the sun was coming up and there wasn't much choice at this point, so the three of us loaded our gear into the canoe and launched it into the surf. Arley would be staying behind. His job was to get a couple of our cousins to meet us when we came back in.

About an hour later, we were maybe half a mile offshore, propelled by my Dad's old 25 horse Evinrude outboard. The sea was calm and the blue-green water was crystal clear. The canoe sat low in the water, weighted down with ice coolers, bait box, a couple of pails of rocks plus two large guys and an outboard engine.

Sweetie and I got busy setting up our fishing tackle. First I grabbed one of our 'ōpelu baitfish and put it on the blade of my paddle, which I had laid across the gunwales to use as a cutting board. I cut the 'ōpelu in half, slitting the fish right up the middle. One half, I cut into pieces. I picked up a rock from a bucket and used the other half of the 'ōpelu to wrap up both the rock and the cut-up pieces of fish. I embedded the huge three inch ahi hook tied to the end of my line into the large piece of 'ōpelu. I tied a slip knot with the line around the whole thing. Sweetie rigged his up the same way. We had done this often before, and it was fast and easy work for us.

I picked up the 400 pound test hand line. It's made up of several lines woven together, with small lengths of string we stuck through it every six feet, each string marking a fathom. We measured this by stretching out a length of the line overhead, with our arms widespread.

That's a fathom. We'd be fishing down between one hundred and two hundred feet.

"No foget, we only got tree hooks, you know, so no spoil 'em eh," I reminded Sweetie. "Tree should be 'nuff if we jus play 'em nice and easy."

I picked up my tackle and dropped it carefully over the side, then started feeding out line with my hands. Sweetie gathered his up and did the same. We could see the tackle descending deeper and deeper into the crystal clear water for a long, long time. We watched it go down until it disappeared from view in the deep.

The rock is a weight. The ahi is a deepwater fish. You need to get down at least 40 fathoms to where he lives. When you get the bait down to where the ahi are, you give your line a jerk. The slip knot opens, and the chum falls into the water. This attracts the ahi. The other half of the 'ōpelu has the hook embedded.

Now, all we had to do was wait. I got a soda from the cooler and lay back in the canoe. I had one leg dangling over the side, and I draped my line over the 'iako. The 'iako is the piece that attaches the outrigger to the canoe. I let the line run over the palm of my left hand. When I had a bite, I was going to know about it right away. I was warm and relaxed and feeling fine. Sweetie sat bolt upright at his end of the canoe trying not to doze off, a loose grip on his line. After a half hour or so, he suddenly jerked awake.

"Uncle!"

I sat up quickly. Sweetie's line was running through his fingers, and it had startled him.

"OK, now give'm some ..."

Before I could say anything more, Sweetie jerked up on the line. And that was that. The line went slack, the fish and one of our precious hooks were gone.

"You gotta give'm slack, brah!" I was trying not to yell at him. I had a lot more to say, but suddenly my own line started to run. I let the fish take a little. The depth of the bait and the strength of the pull of the line told me it was a nice sized ahi.

"Big buggah!" I told Sweetie.

"*Auwē*, ride 'em, Uncle!"

I played the fish for a while, letting out line and pulling it in. When the fish was near the surface, I told Sweetie to get our gaffe ready, and he grabbed it from the bottom of the boat. Our "gaffe" was a baseball bat with a lead weight wrapped around the tip and a big ugly hook protruding from the end.

It took about 20 minutes before the fish tired and finally surfaced. I held the line while Sweetie gaffed him. We got him on board and laid him in the bottom of the boat. I threw some ice from the cooler on the fish. Sweetie and I settled back in opposite ends of the canoe, facing each other. Then we start to laugh, I guess in relief and in triumph.

"Dat one big buggah, dat fish," Sweetie said.

"Dat's not one fish!"

"Look like one fish to me."

"Look like one new clutch to me."

Sweetie laughed.

"You right. And look like one big Christmas pahty for me and my friends. *Mele Kalikimaka*, Uncle!"

But it was time to get back to work.

"OK, put da line back in da wattah," I said. "We gotta catch some mo' fish."

We were in high spirits as we started to re-rig our lines. It was going to be a good day.

It was just past noon when we got back to the beach. We probably looked more like a maritime disaster than a floating canoe. We were sitting so low in the water, the 'iako was nearly awash as we made our way through the tricky shore break. Sweetie and I were singing at the top of our lungs, Christmas carols, and old Hawaiian songs. Sweetie didn't know many of the Hawaiian words, so he filled in the blanks with gibberish and laughter. When we got close into the beach, he gunned the engine and we ran the canoe up on the sand.

I was glad to see that a bunch of my young nephews and cousins were waiting for us. Arley had done his job, as usual. They ran over to give us a hand pulling the canoe up on the beach.

Lopaka was looking into the canoe. "Holy shit, Uncle!"

"Damn!" said another kid.

Seven 50 to 120 pound ahi packed in ice in a twenty four foot canoe are an impressive sight. Sweetie and I climbed out as the boys all gathered around to see what we had brought in.

"We goin' make one big Christmas pahty and all the guys in Kona goin' come!" Sweetie announced.

The young men whooped it up, slapping their new hero, Sweetie, on the back. I guess he was as proud as he'd ever been in his life. But we had to get the ahi onto fresh ice for the trip to the Suisan fish auction on the other side of the island. I reached into the canoe and hauled out a huge fish, picking it up by the tail and pulling it over my shoulder.

"We not goin' have one pahty, if the fish no get to Hilo."

Sweetie, a big grin on his face, leaned casually against a palm tree and let the others carry the fish to my cousin's truck. I grabbed up our empty ice coolers and hauled them over to the trucks. I started loading the coolers with fresh ice, and I called to Sweetie.

"Eh! No only stand around, give me one hand."

Sweetie came over to help me carry the coolers. We set off in the direction of the canoe.

"Where we goin' with dis?" he asked me.

"Gotta load up for the next trip," I told him.

This stopped Sweetie in his tracks.

"Next trip?"

"Da fish still biting out dere. We go get some mo' before everybody else finds out."

Obviously it never occurred to him that we would be going out again. He was ready to spend the rest of the afternoon telling his cousins big game fishing stories and planning for his blowout of a party.

Lopaka saw that I was loading up the canoe.

"Wat, you guys goin' out one mo' time?" he asked.

"Plenny fish out dere still," I said.

"You sure get plenny fish blood in dat canoe. Sharks goin' come."

"Sharks, Uncle!" Sweetie said.

"Da kine, Liko, he wen come back one hour ago. He seen some sharks, fo' sure. He not goin' out again."

"Sharks are our 'aumakua. They're our guardian

angel, brah. No need worry about 'em," I said. Sweetie was looking doubtful so I tried another tack.

"Eh, Sweetie and me, we not afraid of some sharks, right Sweetie?"

As the reigning hero, Sweetie had to go along.

"Shit, no!" he said. "Sharks no scare us."

He called out to the others, those less daring than us.

"Eh, give us one hand with dis canoe! We going back out fo' some mo'." With that bit of bravado, we launched our boat into the surf.

By mid-afternoon. The canoe was very low in the water again, with two 100 pound ahi in ice. I was napping and Sweetie was sulking. I think it had finally hit him that I tricked him into this second trip. We had one line in the water.

"Getting late, Uncle."

"Lissen, if you do what I say and not lose anotah hook, we be outta here by now."

"We no need some mo' fish."

I pointed to our catch. "See that big buggah ovah dere? Dat's my wife's new four piece bedroom set. Queen bed. Headboard. Six drawer bureau. Mirror. And dat other fish, just a little smaller? Dat's her new TV with remote control. And dis other one." I wiggled my hand line. "Dis one is one new Guild 12–string guitah. Dat's fo' me. We get dis one, den we go home. OK?"

"What if we don't get anotah one? We no have bite for ovah one hour. Suppose ...." Our conversation was interrupted by a welcome tug on my line, the unmistakable feel of a good-sized ahi.

"Guitah calling me," I said.

For a couple of minutes, I worked the fish, the line wrapped around my hand. This guy was putting up a struggle. It was my last hook, and I had to be careful not to lose it or the fish.

Then, wham! — there was this huge yank on the line that nearly catapulted me over the bow of the canoe. Sweetie laughed, thinking I was clowning around. I quickly wrapped the line around the 'iako, and the bow was now pulled down into the sea, almost to the water line. Sweetie sobered up quickly.

"Wat the hell was that?" he wanted to know. I was wondering the same thing myself. Now I could see that the canoe was moving. We were being pulled forward.

"Start the engine!" I yelled to Sweetie. Sweetie gave the starter rope a pull, and nothing happened. He gave it another yank, and the old motor sputtered to life.

"Reverse! Put 'em in reverse!" I shouted. Sweetie put it into reverse and opened the throttle, but all this did was lower the bow further, and seawater started to pour in over the sides of the canoe. We were on the verge of sinking in dangerous waters, over a mile from shore.

"No, no, kill 'em, kill 'em!" I yelled. Sweetie shut down the engine. The canoe stabilized. We had taken on a lot of water. We had a couple of empty plastic syrup containers with a rope attached to the handle and the bottom cut off to form a scoop. We immediately grabbed these and started to bail. Glancing behind us, I could see that there was a wake behind our canoe. We were clearly being pulled forwards, and at a pretty good speed.

"Wat the hell is dat?" Sweetie's face had gone pale with fear.

"Ain't no sardine. Swallow that ahi whole, brah," I said, chuckling, with more courage than I really felt. Sweetie peered down into the ocean in front of the boat. Suddenly he pointed downward into the deep.

"Look!"

I looked down into the water, where a tiny gray fish was swimming along just ahead of our canoe. But our fishing line extended all the way from our boat to this "minnow." It was a trick of perspective: the "minnow" was a huge shark, deep in the clear blue water, pulling us along.

"It's one shark! Cut da line!" Sweetie yelled.

"Dat's da last hook!"

"Please, Uncle, you so *pa'akikī*. Cut da line, let's get outta here." *Pa'akikī*. Stubborn. Yeah, I guess that's me, sometimes. But this fish was making me angry.

"He's not getting my last damn hook."

"He's taking us away from land!"

I took my bearings, and sure enough, we were being pulled away from the island. I reached down in the canoe and came up with my home-made gaffe, and hefted it.

"What you goin' do wid dat?"

"Wait fo' him get tired. Den whack 'em on da head when he come up."

Sweetie looked at me in disbelief. Okay, maybe I wasn't being smart about this. But I wanted that guitar. To get the guitar, I needed my hook. All I had to do is get it out of the mouth of the large shark down below us. I settled back into the seat with the gaffe in my lap. I knew this might take some time.

Thirty minutes turned into an hour, and then another hour passed. The canoe was still being pulled along by the shark. The island shore was receding in the distance now, and the sun was much lower on the horizon. I sat with the gaffe at the ready. Sweetie was trying a new tactic, staring me down. It wasn't working.

"You *pupule*, brah," he finally said. I'm not crazy, though. That damn fish was not going to get my last damn hook. We kept moving south. I decided to tell Sweetie a reassuring story. I asked him if he remembered my *Tūtū* Koko'o, my father's grandmother.

"She *pupule* too," he let me know. I used to think so. So I told Sweetie my story. When I was a little guy, maybe three or four years old, my *tūtū* used to take me down to the sea once a month or so on the lava rocks near Kealia. She would pick up a couple of large stones and bang them together, over and over. Eventually, a huge dark shadow would appear in the water. A big shark. And she would start feeding him. She brought whatever she had to give him, usually *'ōpelu*, but sometimes taro, sometimes *'ulu*, cooked breadfruit, whatever she had on the stove in our cookhouse. She'd smile at the shark and chuckle to herself while she'd toss the food out to him. He would swallow the food whole, and swim in circles, looking for more. She'd always remind me that this was the "grandpa shark," the one with all the whiskers.

I was a little kid, and I didn't know any better. I'd never heard of a shark with whiskers, and I wanted badly to see one. The shark would make pass after pass until the food was gone. She'd promise him she would come back soon. She would wave goodbye to the shark and make me do the same. And then she'd take my hand and lead me back on the narrow path up the cliff. Later, when I was a little older, and taking a cue from my big brother, I would just laugh at her when she went off to feed "grandpa." But I really missed those trips to feed him.

Sweetie was listening intently.

"So because I wen make fun of her she nevah take me to feed da shark again."

"How come she feed sharks?"

"You know, I always used to tink about that. I nevah find out fo' one long time, from Uncle Kamuela. You remembah him?"

"Yeah. Had white hair and one cane. I remembah."

"Uncle Kamuela wen tell me dat when *Tūtū* Koko'o was one young kid, she one *pupule* buggah."

"I believe dat."

So I told Sweetie the rest of the story: My uncle told me that back in the 1920's, when *tūtū* was around sixteen, she had been with the family, gathering *'opihi*, a small limpet that clings to the rocks above the sea. The ocean was rough that day, but when the swells receded, they revealed the wonderfully tender yellow-tinged *'opihi*, the ones you usually couldn't get. The ones further out of the water were green and crunchy, still delicious, but, *Auwē!*, those yellows were so good, eaten raw with Hawaiian salt and seaweed. You could only get them on big wave days, 15 or 20 foot surf, when the *'opihi* would climb out of the water a little higher.

Anybody else would wait for a smaller surf day, and gather the *'opihi* when it was safe, but before they moved back down the cliff. Not my *tūtū*. She couldn't wait. She had invented her own system using a couple of 30 foot bamboo poles. One of the poles had a small net attached to the end. The other one had a putty knife tied on the end of it. Hanging out over the cliff, she would pry the 'opihi loose with the knife on the one pole and then flip them into the net on the other pole. She was leaning dangerously close to the pounding surf as she worked. Her mother called out to her to stop, but tūtū had to have those yellows. A stubborn young woman.

Nobody saw her fall, except her little brother. One moment she was there, reaching down over the cliff, and the next moment she was gone. "Sistah wen fall on da rocks," was all little Paloa could say. And she must have hit her head and been knocked unconscious, because she wasn't seen again. Some of the braver young men climbed down towards the water, to try to recover her body. But it was too dangerous with the big surf, and their families pleaded with them until they came back to higher ground. That night, she was mourned with the old Hawaiian chants, her grieving family sitting a vigil by torchlight on the top of the cliff. If she was still alive, the torches would be a sort of lighthouse to guide her home. If she was dead, they would be a beacon for her spirit to see.

They didn't return to the house until after dawn. Tūtū's mother went in first, and a moment later everyone heard a shocked cry from within the house. They rushed inside to find an impossible sight: there was tūtū lying in her bed. She had a huge mark, undoubtedly from the fall into the rocks, from the left side of her face all the way down to her left knee, kind of like a big red birthmark.

Still disbelieving her own eyes, her mother gently touched her daughter, and tūtū opened her eyes. She was alive! It was a miracle. How did she get here? Had she not fallen after all? No, she said, she fell into the water and a shark, a "grandpa" shark with whiskers, carried her to a beach a couple of miles away. She swam to shore, and walked home. No one was there. Exhausted, she fell asleep, awakening to her mother's touch.

Her auntie wanted to clean her wounds, but *tūtū* wouldn't let her, insisting that they were marks of honor, not caused by the rocks, but by a slap from the shark. The "grandpa" shark. It became the standard family joke. From then on, *tūtū* wore her "shark" scar proudly. And she began feeding sharks, from that day until the end of her life more than 70 years later.

"So now you know," I told Sweetie, "Sharks are good luck fo' us." He almost seemed convinced. But it was sunset, and we were now miles from home, with the wind and the currents against us. We knew it was going to be tough getting back.

Just then, the line went slack. I leaned far out over the water, which scared the hell out of Sweetie.

"He's coming up," I said.

I stood up in the canoe and braced myself, holding the gaffe high over my head. My mouth was a little dry. Maybe this hadn't been such a good plan, but even cutting the line wasn't going to help us now. Still, I was determined, if there was a chance, to nail this guy and get my hook back. I must have appeared just a bit crazed, poised there, silhouetted against the setting sun, with this ridiculous looking weapon above my head. Sweetie was looking at me like I was a madman.

And suddenly, he was there, right next to the canoe. He wasn't the biggest shark in the sea, but he wasn't much smaller than our 24 foot canoe, either. He rolled his eyeball back, as sharks do to protect their eyes before they attack. I could see the whites of his rolled back eyes, and I knew he was getting ready to eat. His dorsal fin stood a good three feet out of the water, to our canoe's 12 inches. I got ready to bring my club down on his head. I waited for the perfect position for my blow.

That's when I saw the whiskers. This shark had a beard! But no, it wasn't a beard. It was dozens, maybe hundreds of fishing lines and streams of seaweed coming out of his jaws and mouth. It was only a moment, but I could clearly see lines made of sennet, the old coconut fiber used by Hawaiian fisherman many years ago. For an instant I flashed back to the time with my *tūtū*, feeding the sharks in Kealia.

Distracted by the memory, I hesitated an instant too long, and my opportunity was lost. It was all the time the shark needed to get himself under the canoe, his huge body rocking the boat. Sweetie had a death grip on the *'iako*, his face a mask of pure terror. The outrigger on our left came up and out of the water, and the canoe started to overturn. Unable to keep my balance, I fell towards the shark, turning in mid air and exposing the left side of my body to the shark. If I fell into the sea, I knew I was a dead man. But then his tail came up, and he slapped me hard from head to foot with his rough, barnacled body, knocking me back into the canoe. With a quick and fluid motion, he turned and dove deep, snapping the line at last, leaving Sweetie and me bobbing alone far out to sea at sunset in our tiny craft.

Six hours later, a little past midnight, we finally got back to the beach. The ice had melted long ago, and our catch was spoiled. My entire left side was bruised and swollen from the sharks' rough slap, the scars of which I will bear the rest of my life. Sweetie hadn't spoken a word to me the whole time. He would never go fishing with me again.

I am a modern American who has flown high over the ocean at nearly the speed of sound, and I am an ancient Hawaiian, who travels slowly and low in the sea, not even as high as a shark's fin. I am contemporary Western man as surely as I am my old *tūtū*. I am as stubborn and reckless as she was, and I have seen things she has seen. And my connection to the lives of my ancestors is cemented further, as it has been over and over during the course of my life.

This happened in December, 1976.

Going First

When I started out touring as a professional musician, I had a lot to learn. If you have ever been to one of my performances, you know that you'll always be able to see me, even if I'm not on stage. You'll usually find me in the front of the concert hall at a table, talking story, greeting old friends, signing autographs and selling CDs. And I always ask people to sign my guest book. This is how I make my living, and I work hard at it.

My first gig on my first mainland tour was in San Diego, at a place called Humphrey's. At the time I wasn't a Dancing Cat artist. I had been recording for 20 years with my own recording company, Kealia Farms, and had made a few CDs and cassettes. I had with me 800 CDs, 400 of my CD called *Ho'oilina* with my son and 400 of another, *E Lili'u*.

I was with a couple of other slack key artists who were better known than me. Before the performance, we had a big conversation about the order of our appearance in the show. It was a friendly discussion. We are all good friends who have known each other for years, but business is business. One of the guys was getting twice as much money as me. He was really the star of the show. He felt that as the big name performer he should go on last. That seemed right to me. That left me and the other guy as sort of opening acts, and the other guy sure didn't want to go on first. So finally, I settled it by saying, "I'll go first."

So I went up first and did my set. The audience was a wild crowd. They were drinking a lot of beer, and they were into everything. Some audiences take a while to warm up, but not this bunch. They chanted with me, they clapped, they sang along and with a little encouragement from me, I actually had them howling at the moon.

As soon as I finished my set, a line started in front of the table where I had my CDs displayed, and I started autographing CDs. My friend Kaui Merghart and her husband Maka, and their hula *hālau* danced for me. A *hālau* is like a school or group that teaches and promotes Hawaiian culture, including hula dancing. This was a big *hālau*, and there were about a dozen people dancing in the show.

So when I got off the stage, they started helping me open up wrappers on the CDs. This kept things moving quickly. And I kept on signing through everybody else's set. The crowd was hot for Hawaiian music in San Diego. A big local record store was supposed to come in with the Dancing Cat CDs and set up for the other performers, but they never showed up. I sold all 800 of my CDs and about 250 cassettes, every one I had, in that one night. It was unbelievable.

So I ended up that evening with more than $10,000 in cash, mostly fives and tens, but also everything from ones to hundred dollar bills. It was a huge volume of cash. Now I had to figure out what to do with all this money. The only handy place I had to put it was in my guitar case. I took out the guitar and stuffed the case full of money. I didn't want to carry this much cash on the rest of my gig with me, of course. So the next morning, I walked into the Bank of America across the street with my guitar case full of cash. I thought, this is going to be easy: I'll turn in the money, and they'll give me a cashier's check or something.

It turned out that it was not that simple. The bank turned me down. I went to Wells Fargo and then Sumitomo, same thing. I started going to all the little banks I could find, all the time carrying all these bucks inside my guitar case and hoping that somebody would take the money. It was the same story at every bank. I wasn't a customer, and I didn't look or talk like a local. Maybe they took me for a Colombian. They must have thought it was drug money or something. I should have been smarter and bought a little bag for the money. Finally, I got a friend in San Diego to take the cash off my hands and give me a check.

So that was my first big gig. Now, when we're planning the order of our appearances on stage and someone asks, "Who wants to go first?" I say "Me!" While the other performers are playing on the stage, I'm busy selling all the way through, from the beginning all the way to the end of the concert.

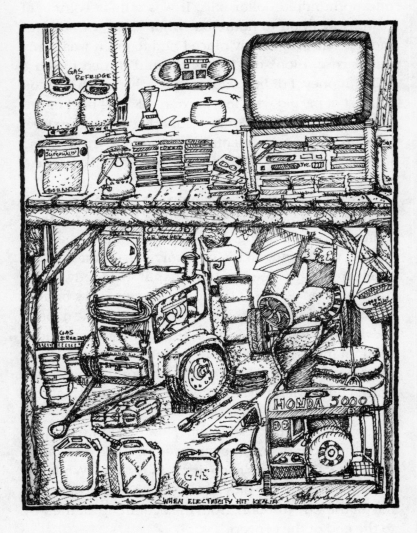

When Electricity Hit Kealia

I have been on TV quite a few times, but I usually didn't get to see myself because for a long time I didn't own a TV set. Actually, there was a good reason for this.

My brothers and I, along with several cousins, had a farm and related businesses when we lived in Kealia, on the Big Island. We decided to build ourselves a pole house in the remote area where the farm was located. This was a 15 year project, with the work done mostly on weekends. We went up to the mountain, cut down 'ōhi'a trees for the posts, took the bark off, and used the tree trunks to build the house. We were also working on the Hyatt doing construction, so we got most of the rest of the lumber we needed from wood that had been used to pour the concrete forms for the hotel. We also got a bunch of lumber from the old Merrie Monarch stage. When we finally got it finished, we had this big old two-story house, about 4400 square feet. We had no electric-

ity, just kerosene lamps and propane gas for the refrigerator.

On the farm we were picking 40,000 ti leaves a week
for the *laulau* market in Honolulu. *Laulau* is a Hawaiian
dish made with meat and fish wrapped in ti leaves. With
four guys, working twelve hours a day, it took us four
days to pick them. Then, we had to go pick up slop to
feed our 1200 pigs. Two, sometimes three times a day,
we would fill up two trucks plus the trailers with meat,
pork, apples, whatever. Our regular slop run included
Burger King, Jack in the Box, all the Chinese restaurants,
McDonald's, all in Kailua, Kona, which is 35 miles away
from our farm. Then we had all these other chores to
get done, feed the pigs, boil the slop, pick coffee, etc.
And we had this additional little enterprise with grain,
too. We would buy a whole container of feed and split it
up, this seventeen thousand dollars worth of grain from
the mainland. It came in once a month, and we sold it
to the other farmers. It's all part of this whole farming
thing.

After a while I had enough money to buy a generator, so I wired the whole house. I got one of those Honda
5000 generators. This thing eats a lot of gas, a gallon an
hour. But you can go four or five hours and not run out
of gas. Once you have electricity, of course, you have to
go and buy a TV. So we went over to General Appliance
in Kealakekua and bought the best TV we could find,
with the biggest screen, I think it was about 27 inches
across. Had surround sound and everything.

Where we lived, there was no cable and we couldn't
catch a signal. When we turned the TV on, all we could
catch was, 'Sssssst'. So we had to buy a VCR. And with

the VCR, we had to go rent some videos, since we didn't own any. At that time I had my three nephews working for me, my cousin Michael, my two brothers and myself. So we figured there's seven of us, you know, so let's see, seven guys, let's let each guy borrow ten videos each. It seems cheap, two dollars a video, what's two dollars, you know? So we go in, and everybody gets ten videos. And we watch everything, from Charlie Chan to Jackie Chan to chicken fights. Everybody's having a great old time.

Right at this same time, I had to go on a performing tour to China. It was a 10 day trip, and I would be playing my music for the Chinese Premier at the opening of the new Sheraton Hotel in Beijing. So I left, looking forward to an interesting trip, thinking my farm was in great hands. Instead, disaster. What happened is that the boys ended up trying to watch all these videos. Unfortunately, they didn't do anything else *but* watch videos. And eventually the generator ran out of gas. You can only go five hours on the five gallon tank.

On the farm we had trucks, we had Bobcats, we had welding machines, we had cement mixers, that all run with gasoline. So the guys started siphoning gas. First they figured, oh, we don't need the welding machine, so they siphoned that out. They got two and a half gallons there. Oh, we don't need the Bobcat, we don't have to scoop up the manure, let's leave that, so they siphoned the gas out. Then, oh, maybe we can siphon some out of the trucks, so they start emptying gasoline out of the tanks. We had four trucks. They siphoned all of the gas out of all the trucks.

When I came back from my China tour, nobody

picked me up at the airport. I had to hitchhike all the way back home. When I reached the farm, the place was a mess. No work had gotten done. Plus, when they ran out of gas from the trucks, nobody picked up the slop for 10 days, so we lost the accounts because the stuff was piling up at Burger King, McDonald's, the Chinese restaurant, and the supermarket, our biggest account.

The pigs never got fed because the slop never got picked up. Meanwhile, a load of feed had come in from the mainland. Because we had no gas in our trucks to go pick it up, a whole container sat on the shipper's truck, and they'd been charging me a hundred bucks a day for storage. On top of that, the ti leaves didn't get sent to Honolulu. We were getting five cents a leaf, so in one week we lost $2,000 just on that.

That was the demise of my farm. I lost all of my accounts. Then I went to return the videos. Nobody stopped to think that when you borrow videos, it's two dollars per day. So here I had 70 videos, out at two dollars per day, for 10 days. I had to pay something ridiculous, like $1,400. You talk about a guy being mad — I was mad. So I sold the TV and the VCR. That was back in '83, and it was many years before I finally bought another TV.

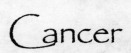

Cancer

Cancer

When I was 27 years old, I woke up one morning and I couldn't walk, my legs were just numb. At first I thought maybe I had a hernia, because one of my testicles was really huge, like the size of a softball. I tried to get out of bed and fell flat on my face. It felt like I was paralyzed from the waist down. My wife Penny called an ambulance and they took me to the hospital in Hilo. The doctor had a look at me and decided to do a surgical biopsy. They gave me a shot that put me out, and that was the end of day one for me.

When I woke up it was around 10 o'clock the next morning, the "softball" was gone and my whole family was there in the room. My wife was there, my mom, my aunties, and all my *hānai* (foster) kids. Their eyes were all full of tears, but no one wanted to say anything. So we all waited until the doctor came.

The doctor showed up about an hour later, making his rounds. He cleared the room and told me the tests confirmed the worst — I had cancer of the testicle. Even worse, all of my lymph nodes were cancerous. This means the cancer had likely spread to the rest of my body. He said that I could try surgery, chemotherapy and radiation, which might prolong my life, but that most times people with my condition live less than six months. I was 27 years old and my son was eight years old. I had a couple of foster kids, Daniel and Patty. And I was going to be dead before the year was out.

At this point my *tūtū* (grandmother) entered the picture. She had already saved my life once, when I was six weeks old. She was like a family healer in a way, and she knew how to interpret dreams. She wasn't like that when she was younger but in her old age she got the gift.

She used to gather seeds. She knew every single tree that gave some kind of seed or fruit or vegetable or medicine on the whole island of Oahu, where she lived. She'd get on the bus and go down to some park, Lili'uokalani Gardens or Kukui Nut Gardens. She knew where all the nuts were, and all about the seeds, the plants and everything growing in the wild. She'd gather all kinds of plants to take home.

She would make leis from kukui and from donkey eye, a vine that grows up tree trunks. Outside it looks really spiny. You don't even want to touch it because it's covered with thin hairs like little needles that will stick you. What you do is hit it with a stick and all the needles and the seeds fall off and the nuts come out. The seeds are what she used to make the leis.

Tūtū had quite a production going. She gathered shells, which she kept in gallon bottles in her house. It looked like the home of a sorceress, with bottles of seeds and shells, leis and all kinds of rocks filling up the place.

Now that I think about it, in a way it's kind of like my classroom today, where you'll find bottles of dried *māmaki, koko'olau, uhaloa, 'awa, hawiwi, kukui, imu* stones and other stuff.

My *tūtū* lived on Oahu, and I was in the hospital in Hilo. Distance did not present a problem for her. She called everybody and said, "Look, we're going to do something called *kūkulu kumahana*, which is where you join the life forces. Everybody's going to fast and pray together." This is called *ho'okē ai*.

So my family called all my other relatives, and lots of friends, too, wherever they were. The word went out mostly by telephone, passed all over the place. Everybody told everybody else, *"Tūtū's* calling for a fast for George. Please help him out." They all fasted for five days. While this was going on, my *tūtū* had me take a Hawaiian herbal medicine called *kauna'oa*. It's made from three ingredients, all called *kauna'oa*. There's a plant that grows on the beach, kind of an orange vine. And then there's *kauna'oa*. that lives in the sea. It's like a white string, a kind of star fish. And then there's another *kauna'oa*. that grows on the mountains. It looks like barbed wire, but it's tougher. You take the three things, coming from the mountain, from the beach and from the ocean, burn them into ashes and make a tea and drink it for five days.

By the end of the fifth day there were probably 2,000 to 3,000 people fasting, my whole family, aunties, uncles, cousins, my brothers — wherever they were. My mom said that Nappy Pulawa and the Hawaiians in jail at McNeil Island Penitentiary in Tacoma, Washington were praying for me too.

On the morning of the fifth day a phone call at about six o'clock in the morning awakened me from a very deep dream. It was my *tūtū* over on Oahu. She said, "Well, Keoki, I know you had a dream." I said, "Yeah, it was a beautiful dream." She said, "Tell me about your dream."

So I started describing my dream to her. There was this black sand beach that went for miles, like Kalapana black sand beach in Puna District on the Big Island of Hawai'i. I was walking along the beach and not paying attention too well and all of a sudden there was this huge wave. It knocked me to the ground, to my hands and knees. She asked, "Did the wave cover your whole body?" I said, "Yeah, I was drowning in this big wave. It receded though." She said, "Oh, that's good, that's a good sign."

I told her that when the wave receded, there were all these fish flopping around on the black sand beach. She asked, "What did you do next?"

"Well, I climbed a coconut tree I busted some coconut leaves and wove a basket," I told her.

"And next?" she asked.

"Oh, *tūtū*, there were so many fish on that beach, that I just filled up that basket as full as I could carry, there were millions and millions of fish."

"What did you do next?" she asked me.

"I went down the street, walking along, and whoever I met I just gave them some fish."

"What kind of fish was it?" she wanted to know.

"You know, *tūtū*, my dad was a fisherman and I know fish, but I've never seen this kind of fish in my life. They were silver and long and flat instead of having a round body. Pure silver on two sides. Tons of them, but I only could carry so much in the basket."

"What happened next?" she asked.

"Well, I reached home. I didn't know what home it was but it felt like home at the end of the road. All I had was six fish left. The scene changed then. All of a sudden I was sitting before this huge bonfire that was going off and in my hand I had a *pū'olo*." A *pū'olo* is like a little *laulau*, a ti leaf wrapping for gifts.

"And," I went on, "I was trying to decide if I wanted to throw this *pū'olo* into the fire or not."

She said, "Wow, and what happened next?"

I said, "That's when the telephone rang and you woke me up from the dream."

"Oh," she said, "A beautiful dream!"

So I said, "*Tūtū*, tell me what it means."

She said, "This is your dream: The blackness of the sand is like all the *kaumaha*, the heavy load, the trouble you're having right now with your work because a lot of people who claim to help you out are jealous of the things that you're doing. They don't want you to succeed. That's the blackness, the darkness. But also there is evil around you. The evil is the cancer in your body. The wave that knocked you to the ground is the hand of God. And the fact that he covered your whole body with seawater is like he baptized you."

Hawaiians believe that salt is a blessing. We bless our homes by spraying ocean salt water on them. My *tūtū* went on, "When this water receded what God left behind was his blessings in the form of the fish. Millions of blessings. You could only take so much 'cause your basket was full. And what you did with your blessings, you didn't keep them to yourself, you gave them away to everyone you met along the road. The six fish that were left in the basket means that in six weeks you will be cured. Not six months, six weeks. You're not going to die but be cured.

"When you stood before the fire with the *pū'olo* you didn't know what to believe in. The *pū'olo* is all the things about our past. If you throw it in the fire you get rid of it. If you hold onto it, that's going to be part of what you hold onto. That part you have to discover for yourself. What you're going to keep and what you're going to forget about our past. You must choose and take the best of two worlds, from Western culture and from your Hawaiian culture."

She really believed I was going to be cured in six weeks. "Should I go through surgery and chemotherapy and radiation or not?" I asked her.

She said, "Go through radiation therapy and chemotherapy and surgery not to satisfy me, or God, but to satisfy your mom, your aunties and your wife. You should do that because if you didn't try everything, they'd still think, 'Oh, he should have done this or that.' The Hawaiian medicine is working already. This chemotherapy cannot hurt. We'll do everything, Hawaiian way and Western way. This way you'll have the best of two worlds."

So that's what I did. I flew over to Honolulu and started treatment at a hospital there. Every day I went to chemotherapy. When I first began, I could see on the x-rays that my lymph nodes were all white throughout my body. All the valves, anything that has a valve, like the one that cuts all the acids to my stomach were white. I had several surgeries, and I've got all these operation scars on my body. They took out two-thirds of my stomach, one testicle, and radiated my thyroid.

At four weeks they did some testing, and a funny thing happened. At the same time another George Kahumoku was in the same hospital: my dad, George Kahumoku, Sr. was there because of a leaky heart valve. And when they looked at my x-rays, there was nothing there, the cancer didn't show up at all. They knew this couldn't be right, the cancer couldn't just disappear. They figured that they had gotten my x-rays mixed up with my dad's. So they did two more weeks of testing. And almost to the day that I went into the hospital at six weeks, they said, "This guy's clear, get him out of here." So I was back in Hilo exactly six weeks from the day my tūtū said.

I guess you can conclude whatever you want from this story. If you want to believe in Western medicine, you can say that it was the chemotherapy and other treatments that cured me. If you want to believe in the Hawaiian medicine, you can believe that. For me, I think it doesn't matter. I believe that just as I am a product of two different cultures, I can be influenced and maybe cured by both.

Even today, I still choose the best from each culture, Western and Hawaiian. I believe that they can compliment each other, as Auntie Edith Kanaka'ole and my tūtūs taught me. I'm sure glad that when I had cancer I didn't have to do one without the other.

Keoki's Debut

Back in 1990, I was playing with my brother Moses at the Mauna Kea Beach Hotel on the Big Island. Moses and I didn't always see eye to eye, and pretty soon it became a solo act — me. The hotel put up with it for a while, but they had contracted to hear two Kahumoku's, not a soloist. Finally, they got tired of it and they gave me a week to find another performer to play with me, or I'd be fired.

I was in a tough spot. The Mauna Kea was a great, steady gig, and it would be hard times if I lost the job. I couldn't find anybody else who I could count on to play with me on a regular schedule. Finally, I decided it would have to be my son, Keoki. He was only 19 years old, working as a house painter, but I figured he could accompany me on the ukulele. All he knew how to do at the time was strum a few chords, but we had played together at family gatherings and it seemed to be all right.

Keoki didn't want to do it. He knew he couldn't play that well, and he didn't want to get up in front of a bunch of people and look like a fool. Finally I convinced him that he would be okay if we practiced together for a while, and if he just followed my lead like he did in back-yard parties with friends and family. So I went out to Hilo Hattie's and bought us a couple of matching aloha shirts. We would be the Kahumoku Family Musicians instead of the Kahumoku Brothers.

It was a pretty busy week for both of us with the farm and other things, and we never did get around to practicing. Before we knew it, it was time to go and play our first gig. It was a clambake at the hotel, outdoors next to the beach. There was a huge stage raised about three feet above the audience. They had this incredible sound system. There were 400 people in the crowd as we stepped up onto the stage, the sun setting behind us.

The audience started to quiet down and pay attention when they noticed us arranging ourselves on the stage. The quieter they got the more nervous Keoki became as he looked out over all those people. He was beyond nervous, he was sweating his guts out. His new shirt was soaked and his hands were dripping. He tried to get out of it one last time. He said, "You know, Dad, I don't know how to play." I said, "That's all right, fake it, just to help out your Dad." I hated to do this to him, but I really needed this job and there was no other way.

Finally it was time, and we started to play. And on the very first strum Keoki's ukulele slipped out of his sweaty hands, bounced off the top of a speaker, and landed in the audience. I stopped playing and for a moment the place was silent. I looked over at Keoki and I could see the panic in his eyes. I knew he was thinking about making a run for it.

We sat motionless for a moment or two, I guess. It

seemed like longer. Then, somebody in the audience laughed, then another person, and then they all started to applaud. I smiled and waved. Keoki was frozen with panic, so I jumped down off the stage and went out into the audience and picked up the ukulele. By this time, everyone thought it was part of the show and we got a standing ovation while I climbed back onto the stage and put the ukulele back into my son's shaking hands.

So that was the opening of his first song as a professional performer. I knew that if he didn't get past that first number, I'd never be able to call on him again. I'd be out of a job at the Mauna Kea. The audience finally sat down and we started to play our first song.

That's when I realized that the flying ukulele was just part one of the disaster. Part two was when Keoki actually began to play. He had learned really strictly how to play … one-two, one-two … kind of real systematic like he learned in high school. He was playing like that and throwing me off.

Just when I was figuring out how to adjust the tempo so we could play together, part three of the disaster: He opened his mouth to sing. What came out was what he had learned in church and school choir. It was kind of operatic, I guess. It was not much like slack key. He was really bad, and it was very distracting.

It seemed like forever, but we finally got to our mid-show break. I grabbed Keoki's ukulele and took it down behind the stage where nobody could see what I was doing. I used my wire cutters and clipped each of the strings on his instrument. Then I used some clear tape to tape the strings down so from a distance, you couldn't see that they weren't connected to anything. The other thing I did was switch off his microphone. Talk about faking it, this was really faking it. But it worked. *Now*, I figured, we were really the Kahumoku Family Musicians.

But my son sure didn't think so. By the time the show ended he was really mad at me. He told me he had never been so embarrassed in his life. He said he was never going to do this again. That would have been the end of the Kahumoku Family Musicians, but before he could stalk away, I handed him $100 in cash.

"What's this for?" he asked me.

"That's your pay," I told him. "We get $300 a night for this gig." You have to understand that this was really good money for us in those days. It sure got his attention. I guess he hadn't realized how much you could make playing music. He didn't say he would ever play again, but he took the cash. I was pretty sure right then that he would be back for our gig on the following night, and he was.

So instead of the end of the Kahumoku Family Musicians, that was the beginning. I started bringing out the song books so he could follow along. After about six months, I reattached one of the strings to his ukulele. At about nine months, after he mastered his one string, I gave him a second string. It took about two years for him to end up with all four strings.

His playing gradually got better over the next year, but he still wasn't playing at what I would call a professional level. This started to change when we moved to Maui. He was married now, and had a kid. He thought he should be paid half of what we were making on the gigs.

I told him, "You start playing half of the music, and carry half the load, and I'll pay you for it." Right about then my brother Moses started living at Keoki's house. I really didn't know how to teach my son to play, but Moses taught him harmonics and all the different stuff you have to know. My brother is an excellent picker and arranger of music. With that help, Keoki just bloomed and blossomed. He really became serious about his music.

Now, I consider him to be a master ukulele and slack key guitar player. That's his story. He didn't start off all nice and rosy, and his first gig was a disaster. But when he made up his mind to become a professional musician, he really did it. I guess I kind of threw him into the water so he would learn how to swim. Maybe it's not the best way to teach somebody, but he sure did learn. I love it now when we put on our matching aloha shirts and take to the stage. I'm very proud of him.

A Fishy Hotel

I grew up in kind of rustic surroundings. Nobody in my family ever had much money, and I am pretty used to raising and hunting my own food and cooking it over an open fire.

In the early seventies, when I built my first house in Kona, I had a big fight with my wife (this was wife number two, Malama) about bathrooms. I had planned for a nice four-hole outhouse perfectly located just outside the back door (but not too close). She wanted to have a toilet right in the house! I finally had to give in. It was my first house with a flush toilet.

In 1992, I was farming in Kona and playing music with my son, Keoki, at the Mauna Kea Beach Hotel. The Mauna Kea is a five star hotel, and they paid us really well. Then they decided to shut it down in the beginning of November for a year for renovations, so we were going to lose that income.

That was kind of painful. Even though I considered myself a farmer more than a musician, it was going to be tough getting along without the extra money from playing music. To be honest with myself, I guess I was making money playing music so I could lose it on the farming. I had other gigs besides the Mauna Kea, but that one was the one that really paid good money.

There was a guy named Steve Shalit who used to be with the Mauna Kea Beach Hotel, and now he was General Manager at the Westin at Ka'anapali on Maui. He heard that my son and I were going to be out of a job in a couple of weeks, so he invited us to come over to Maui.

I couldn't imagine leaving the farm, but this guy kept insisting. He told us that no one was playing Hawaiian music in Ka'anapali. Everything was reggae and other "island" music, but not from our islands. He really liked the stuff he used to hear me play at the Mauna Kea, real Hawaiian music.

He asked us to come over to try it out for a couple of weeks, see if we liked it there. Finally, we agreed to come over for a weekend. He flew us in with our wives, paid for the plane tickets and everything. We arrived at the Kapalua airport, and there was a big limo there to take us to the hotel. I have to say, we enjoyed that. We stayed in a really nice room at the hotel. Everything was on the house. We had all this food, all these free lunches, the seafood buffet — it was great. At night we played music.

But on Monday, we had to go back to Kona. There were 4,000 ti leaves to pack every week, 1,200 pigs to feed, and all kinds of other stuff to take care of on the farm. We were used to working 20 hours a day. The guy from the Westin wanted us to come back to Maui as soon as possible, and we said, "Yeah, yeah, we'll call you back." But I knew I was never going to call him back because how could I leave my farm, how could I leave my coffee, my ti leaves and 1,200 pigs?

Right about this time I had trouble with one of my big boars. I was in the pen with him one morning, and instead of mounting one of the sows, he decided to try to mount me. This kind of thing happens once in a while, and I was carrying a pole with a wire loop on the end. It's a pretty standard device for controlling an uncooperative animal.

When I tried to get the wire loop around his head, the wire got caught on his tusk. He started whipping his head from side to side trying to shake the thing off, and he jerked the pole out of my hand. This was an 800 pound animal, and he was furious. I was trying to get hold of the pole, and I got hit hard in the arms with it several times before I finally got him under control. I was pretty bruised up, but hell, that's farming for you.

About ten days later, a couple days after Thanksgiving, I was getting ready to feed my pigs, carrying four five-gallon buckets of slop, two in one hand two in the other. All of a sudden I couldn't feel anything, my arms went numb, boom! I dropped the buckets I was carrying in my left hand. Then I started feeling very dizzy, and I put everything down and sat on the ground.

I tried to get up, but I couldn't do it. The pigs knew it was time to eat, and that I had the food. I can usually feed my whole herd in less than 20 minutes. Now I was sitting there next to the pens, with 1,200 pigs screaming and yelling for their food.

Fortunately, I had lots of my *'ohana*, my family, around the place. My niece, Pomaikai'i, was feeding some other pigs but she noticed all the noise and came over to see what was going on. She saw me sitting on the ground, and she said, "Uncle are you all right?"

I said, "Yeah," and I tried to stand up one more time. This time I fell flat on my face. I just couldn't get up. My niece ran and got some of my cousins. They carried me to the car and drove me to the hospital.

The doctors did a bunch of tests and found out that a blood clot from my arm had traveled and stuck itself in the right side of my neck and I had an aneurysm. I was in the hospital for a couple of weeks. For a while, I had no feelings in my left hand, and my speech was slurred. My cousins were covering my music gigs for me, but I was getting kind of worried about how I was going to play music.

As soon as I got out of the hospital, I started trying to play music again. I knew I would have to find a way to do it. At first I couldn't even hold up a guitar. What I did was put my arm and hand in a sling so I could hold up the instrument, but I could only play with two fingers on my right hand. I had to re-learn how to play with just the two fingers. It took some practice, but I finally taught myself some new techniques, and pretty soon I could play about everything I needed to play. After a while I began to get the use of all of my fingers back. (To this day, I still play with just two fingers sometimes).

The doctor said I couldn't keep up the kind of activity I was doing. He told me if I didn't change my lifestyle I was going to die. So from the hospital I called the guy from the Westin back and told him we'd come over at the beginning of the year.

On December 25, I got out of the hospital. I told Keoki we'd plan on going over for a month and check things out. I had already started turning over the farm operation to my nephews. So in January of 1993, we moved into a beautiful room overlooking the ocean on the 11th floor of the Westin Ka'anapali Hotel on Maui.

My son and I lived in the hotel for about six months, commuting home by plane to be in Kona on Sunday and Monday. It was a little strange because we were the only native Hawaiians staying in this huge 750 room hotel. It's a pretty expensive place, and as rooms were rented they kept moving us from one room to another.

Each time we moved into a new room, we would take the chips, expensive tins of nuts and the fancy chocolates out of the mini-bar and replace it with our own snacks: seaweed from the rocks near the hotel, sea urchins, poi, and other stuff we liked to eat.

As we moved around over the months we were there, we were moving lower and lower in the hotel. After six months our room was on the fourth floor overlooking the parking lot. We had come down a little over one floor a month. Whenever we moved, we couldn't help noticing the differences in luggage. Everybody else had Gucci or at least Samsonite. Our stuff was carried around in plastic buckets and grocery shopping bags. These were pretty nice digs, though, and we enjoyed the luxury accommodations. But right about then we made a series of big mistakes that would cost us our fancy living.

We played music afternoons and nights. We had a gig at lunchtime, at poolside from three to five in the afternoon, and in the restaurant at night from six to nine. Even though our farm was on another island, we were still farmers, and we would wake up at 5:30 every morning. Then we'd get bored, because we didn't have anything to do. To pass the time, Keoki and I used to go out and walk along the beach. We started collecting the stuff we found. Among other things, we got over 100 snorkels and dozens of mismatched fins. Once we found a hundred dollar bill.

We had the place pretty much to ourselves at that hour. We were walking by Black Rock in front of the Sheraton Hotel one morning when we noticed a big school of *manini*. It's like a striped surgeon fish, and we like to eat that either dried or *pūlehu* (broiled) or *lāwalu* style (roasted) on an open fire.

In Kona we were farmers, but we were also fisherman going back for many generations. We know how to go after all kinds of fish, and we had brought our nets over from the Big Island. We went back to our hotel and got our fishing gear and a bag of frozen peas from the kitchen staff. Keoki and I walked down the beach carrying our white plastic buckets and our nets and returned to Black Rock.

We climbed up on the rock and started tossing the peas into the water. Pretty soon the fish started feeding and we had them in a nice ball. My son threw the net on top of the school, and we waded into the water. Keoki had covered the whole school and we ended up with four five-gallon buckets full of fish. This was a lot more fish than we really needed, but in Hawai'i, we don't waste food. So we took the fish back to our room. This was our first big mistake.

It was still pretty early in the hotel, so we went down to the ground floor and swiped some of the rocks used for landscaping around the hotel pond. They were always trimming trees around the place, and we got some kiawe wood that was lying around. This is mesquite, and is great for barbequing. We took all this stuff back to our room and laid out a little campfire with the rocks in a circle on our balcony so we could cook some fish. I guess this was Big Mistake #2.

I suppose we should have cleaned our catch by the ocean but we knew that the tourists were used to watching the fish when they snorkeled. We didn't think they would like to see us gutting and cleaning fish they thought of as pets or part of the scenery, not food. We really didn't have a proper place to clean all the fish, so we cleaned them in our bath tub. Big Mistake #3. It took quite a while to clean them all, and by the time we were done the drain in our bath tub wasn't working too well. We found out later that the drains for a good part of the hotel were all plugged with fish guts. It was pretty horrible.

So now we had a bathtub full of fish. We sliced them in half down the middle, and we salted them down. We strung lines all throughout our hotel room. We got clothes pins and hung the fish up on lines to dry. Big Mistake #4. We weren't really aware of the odors building up in the room. By this time, not just the room, but the whole damn hall smelled like fish.

While the fish were drying, we lit off our fire. We took the wire shelf from our mini-bar refrigerator and laid it across the rocks for a barbeque grill. We had to wait for the fire to burn down to get some good coals for cooking. We were still pretty sandy from the fishing expedition, and the tub was full of fish guts that weren't draining too well, so we went down to the hotel pool to take a dip and clean ourselves off. We took our time, because we knew it was going to be a while before the wood burned down enough for cooking.

On our way back to our room we noticed all this action going on in front of the hotel. There was an ambulance, police cars and a fire engine. We didn't realize at first that there was any connection with us. To make a long story short, just for this little old campfire, the fire department had busted out their big hose to put out the fire. In fact, they hit the thing with so much water, they washed the whole campfire right off the balcony, and almost broke the windows, too.

At this point, the hotel's assistant manager showed up. He's the guy who's in charge of the rooms. He can't believe what's going on. The whole hotel smells like fish, there's fire hoses and water, and the hotel drains are all plugged up. I told him the story of what happened, that we were just trying to cook some fish. In the end, we got kicked out of the hotel. And later on, Big Mistake #5: we found out that the area in front of Black Rock was some kind of marine sanctuary, and if you fish there it's a $10,000 fine.

We moved out of the hotel two days later, back to more familiar surroundings for us, the Honokohau Valley at the 36 mile marker on the North shore of Maui. Sometimes it's hard for the native Hawaiian to live in the regular world.

He Had a Dream

He Had a Dream

I don't know if you believe in dreams. For me, one of them turned out to predict my future. For years, I kept a journal of all my dreams. In 1972 when I was living in California, I had a dream. First, there was the smell and feel of the ocean. Then I saw a bunch of kids wearing shorts, no shirts on. They were down at a beach building stone walls. That's it, just this kind of scene of kids at a beach in Hawai'i. It didn't mean a lot to me at the time, but the dream was very vivid and the image stayed with me for a long time before it faded from my memory.

I suppose I figured the dream had something to do with my desire to work with kids, which I'd had for a long time. When I was growing up, I was one of the older kids in a large family with lots of cousins. I had a lot of baby sitting responsibilities. There is a Hawaiian family tradition that the older members teach and pass along knowledge to the younger members. Maybe this is where my instinct to teach children comes from.

In California, I was working with a group of dropout kids. Since my background was in art, I was teaching them the basics of painting and we were doing murals all around Oakland. I had gotten some money from a federal program by writing a grant request. It turned out I was pretty good at writing grants, so I did a number of these. But what I really enjoyed was working with the kids.

Finally, an opportunity came to work with kids back in Hawai'i. The principal of a Kamehameha School had heard about my work in Oakland. I was a graduate of Kamehameha, which was set up so that native Hawaiian children could get a good education. She was so impressed by what I was doing, that she came all the way to California to interview me. Then she invited me to come back to Honolulu to take a job with Kamehameha Schools.

I was really happy to be going back home, and with the idea that I was finally going to be able to fulfill what seemed like my destiny. My wife and I packed up and moved to Oahu as soon as we could. But when we got there, we had a surprise. The job had changed from the one they had offered me in California. The position they had was not something I wanted to do. I was pissed, and I turned the job down.

I guess I acted a little impulsively. Now all my stuff was on the wrong island, and I not only didn't have a teaching job, I didn't have any job. I had a wife and a young son and no job, no money, no place to live. The only thing we could think of to do was pack up and move over to Hilo, where my wife's family lived. We moved into a house her parents owned. I needed to find some work in a hurry. I had learned to weld by making metal sculptures and this turned out to be a valuable skill. I got a job as a journeyman welder at the sugar mills.

It wasn't art and it wasn't teaching, but the money was sure good. Sugar prices were really high then, and they needed parts from some old mills to be moved to operating mills. I worked on this demolition crew. We took apart the old mills and they trucked away tanks, pipes and other parts. Mostly I worked in Ka'u, about an hour and a half outside of Hilo. I did this for nearly two years, and made enough money to buy our house and even to buy a second one. Then that job was over, and I ended up on unemployment. I didn't know what I wanted to do with my life then. I had all this background in art and education, but no opportunity to do the kind of work I wanted to do.

I didn't know it at the time, but my application to Kamehameha schools was still on file. A guy named Fred Cachola from Kamehameha School Extension Division heard about me and had a look at my record. They were looking for a principal for a brand new alternative school in Kona. They didn't even have any classrooms built. They wanted someone with experience in grant writing who liked to work with kids.

Fred contacted me, and asked if I would be interested in the job. I told him that I really wasn't sure. This was school administration, not something I really wanted to do. He asked me to go and have a look at the place and talk to the people there. It didn't sound too promising, but a job was a job. I figured I could drop in on my Uncle Pila while I was there, so the trip wouldn't be a total waste of time. So on a rainy Hilo morning in April, I got up early and drove over to the Kona sunshine to visit with my uncle and to take a look at this school.

The school was located right on the beach at Hōnaunau, next to the City of Refuge National Park. This was Bishop Estate land, which had been dedicated to National Park use. When I got there, I found out why they were willing to give the land back to us for the school. I drove down this rough road from the National Park to the school location, only to find the road blocked by a huge truck.

It turned out that this was an overgrown piece of property that had been used as a dumping ground for junk cars for many years. The Army Corps of Engineers was there with a huge forklift, dragging these old cars out of the bushes and stacking them onto this big truck. They had the road completely blocked. I backed up the road and parked my car back in the National Park lot, and walked down towards the beach.

As I came around the last bend in the road, there was the wonderful smell of the ocean, and then a sight that changed my life. There on the beach in front of me were about 60 or 70 kids working on a stone wall. They were swarming all over the thing, pulling out the stones to get rid of the weeds and night blooming cirrus, and then rebuilding the wall. The kids were dressed only in shorts and no shirts.

I had forgotten about the dream by then, but it came flooding back to me at that moment. I was glad I was alone right then, because it would have been difficult to explain to someone else what I was feeling. I just stood there and cried. I knew I had found my life's path. I didn't hesitate for a moment. I took the job, and I've been working with kids ever since.

Looking for Grandfather

"THE PAPAYAS WERE TALL"

Looking for Grandfather

When I think of my Grampa Tommy, the picture that comes to my mind is one from my childhood. I always recall the way he walked. I remember him as a small, yellow-tanned man, maybe five feet one inches tall. He would step along with his back erect, but with his head bowed far down as if he was looking at a point somewhere just ahead of his shoes. He would always hold his hands clasped behind his back. There was purpose in his stride and posture, but somehow the look of a lost soul in his bowed head.

Thinking about it now, I suppose he was kind of a lost soul. He had come alone from the Philippines as a young man, to work in the sugar cane fields and ranches of the Big Island. He had no family in Hawai'i. On weekends, he used to go to the Filipino dance halls with other young men, hoping to find a wife there. Unlike the Japanese workers, who sent home for their brides, these guys were on their own. Tommy didn't find a mate until 20 years later, when he met my grandmother.

Tommy was not my "real" grandfather. He was what

we call in Hawai'i my *hānai* grandfather. He moved in with my widowed grandmother when she was nearly sixty years old, at her house in Kealia, in South Kona, on the Big Island. Since Tommy was only about 45 at the time, this caused some bad feelings in my family. Some of my grandmother's children were not happy with their mother being in bed with a man their own age. But Tommy and my grandmother stayed together for more than 20 years. He cared for my *tūtū*, my grandmother, through all of her various illnesses as she approached the age of 80. You'd think that after so many years the family would accept that they really loved each other. But my family's hostility towards Tommy never went away.

When we were between about two and nine years old, my older brother Van and I used to spend summers with my *tūtū* and Grampa Tommy. Our parents were living in Honolulu. I guess they wanted us to experience life back in Kona. That's where we were from originally. Maybe also it was a break for them to get us out of the house.

Van and I were real terrors. Mostly, we were just a couple of homesick little kids, and we couldn't wait to get back on the airplane that had brought us, and fly home. Van had a very inventive mind, and he could think of a lot of ways for us to get into trouble. There was a lot of scrap wood laying around *tūtū's* house because all of the cooking was done outdoors on a wood fire. Van got the idea to build our own airplane using some of this wood and fly it to Honolulu.

We spent weeks constructing the thing. It had a propeller and two seats, one for me and one for my brother.

We really thought it would fly. But before we got a chance to make a test flight, Van got an even better idea. Some coconut trees had been cut down near our house, and Van was sure that if we tied the fronds to our bodies like bird feathers, we could flap our "wings" and fly home. We gathered up leaves and attached them to ourselves with twine. Van figured we should climb up the 10 foot ladder attached to the water tank to get some height for the launch. I was really happy when he said I could go first. All I can say about my "flight" is that lava rocks can really make you bleed, especially when you hit them head first.

So we didn't get to flap home that summer. The one thing that made Kona bearable for us was Grampa Tommy. He worked hard on McCandless Ranch as the gardener and caretaker, but he always seemed to have time for us. After work and on weekends he would show us how to rope and tie knots, how to play cards, how to light a cowboy match to start the kerosene stove fire going.

He knew all about the plants growing in the forest, and he would take us on long walks so we could pick herbs which we could dry and make into a tea. He showed us how to build a washtub base fiddle using an old galvanized tub, a broomstick and nylon rope from fishing lines. He let us light the fire under the tub so we could take a warm bath. He showed us how to use the inside of sticky bean pods to stick empty tin cans to our feet so Van and I would be several inches taller when we walked. He took us swimming nearly every day, and all the while, told us story after story.

But the thing I remember above all was his music.

Grampa Tommy was a master of the ukulele, guitar, tenor guitar, banjo and mandolin. He had a unique, rhythmic style of playing, maybe from the Philippines. He also had a little sound box that he could plug in to amplify the music. His instruments and sound box were with him wherever he went. He was a quiet man with outsiders, but in much demand to play at parties, weddings, luaus, etc. Van and I spent hours listening to him play, and enjoying his wonderful music.

His real name was Tommy Martinez. *Tūtū* called him "*Ei Nei*," which is an old Hawaiian name that roughly translates as "sweetheart." I remember when he came home from work, how happy she was to see him. She would call out to him in her sing-song voice, "*Ei Nei!* How you?" This name kind of stuck to him. Most people didn't even know his real name, and they called him *Ei Nei.* My brother and I worshipped him. To us, he was simply Grampa.

Many years later, after I went off to college on the mainland, word reached me that my *tūtū* had died. I couldn't afford the fare back home to attend the funeral. When I finally did move back to the Big Island, I found out that some of my family members had taken advantage of the opportunity to kick Grampa Tommy, now in his sixties, out of the house. Nobody seemed to know what had become of him.

I was pretty busy with my move back from the mainland, starting a new career, building a home, raising a family. But I was determined to find Grampa Tommy and I asked about him everywhere I went. Finally I picked up a rumor that he was still in the Kona area, picking coffee. I was living in Hilo then, but I drove over to Kona right away. Workers on the coffee plantation there told me that he had been there, but it had been about a year before. He could pick coffee OK, but he couldn't handle the coffee bags, which weighed between 100 and 120 pounds each.

So my grandfather had moved on, and nobody knew where. At about this time, I moved from Hilo to Kona, and I thought it might now be easier to search for him. But the trail had gone cold. Over a year went by, and I had moved back to Hilo again, because of my job. I was the Hawaiian Islands Coordinator for Alu Like, a Native Hawaiian corporation.

That's when I picked up another rumor. Someone was sure they had seen Grampa Tommy in Waipi'o, working taro. I went right over there, a couple of hours drive. Nobody there knew about any Tommy Martinez, but when I asked for *Ei Nei*, "sweetheart," it was, "Oh, yeah, that old Filipino guy, play music." An old man named Takeo told me about Grampa Tommy. "He was here, but he gone, brah. Taro too heavy for 'em, brah." He had worked taro for six months, but carrying bags weighing 80 to 100 pounds through the mud of the field had been too much for him. *Ei Nei* was trying to earn a living as he had first done over 40 years before, as a young, strong man. He was finding it tough. People remembered him for his music, and everybody remembered his name, "sweetheart." But nobody knew where he'd gone. He had last been seen maybe six months or a year before.

Weeks went by and I followed up on several more rumors. I found a place where Grampa Tommy had worked not too long before, picking papaya. Papaya was carried in 20 pound boxes, which he could handle. The workers pulled the fruit out of the trees using a long bamboo pole with a toilet plunger attached to the end. Sometimes the trees aren't very tall. But here, the trees were big. Working the poles up 20 feet or more into the trees, he'd hurt his neck, and couldn't pick fast enough. Once again, everyone remembered him for his wonderful music. But now he was gone, nobody knew where.

It was a couple of months later, on a rare sunny morning in Hilo, when I decided to take advantage of the fine weather to go for a swim before work at Waipuna cold pond, next to the Hukilau Hotel, over by the old Dairy Queen. I was driving through Hilo at about five thirty or six that morning when I passed an old man walking along the side of the road. Subconsciously, something about him registered: a steady gait, a bowed head, hands clasped behind the back. I couldn't see the man's face.

I pulled over to the side of the road to let him catch up to me, still a little unsure until I got a good look at him. He passed by the car, head bowed, but I knew it was him. "Grampa," I called to him. He stopped and looked into the car, kind of startled. He didn't seem to know me. "Hey Grampa, remember me?"

He studied my face for a moment, then broke into a big grin that brought me right back to my childhood.

"Georgie Boy," he said. He walked over to the car, and I could see the tears in his eyes. Mine were kind of teary, too. He put his rough-skinned old hand on my arm. "Georgie," he said again.

It turned out that he was on his way to work, about a four mile walk. He was living in a boarding house in

Hilo and working at a place just out of town. They raised fish in a pond and then cooked and served them right there fresh in a restaurant right next to the pond. *Ei Nei* had been hired because he knew how to prepare sticky rice on a stovetop better than any cook they'd ever had. He would come in early in the morning, start the rice cooking, and then sweep and mop the floors and clean the bathrooms. At the end of the workday, he would walk back home to his little room in Hilo. He was playing music once a week at the Salvation Army retirement home in town.

We had a basement in our house, and I asked Grampa Tommy to move in with us. He wouldn't do it though — he was too independent. It took me six months of coaxing before he finally agreed to live with my wife Penny and my son Keoki and me.

I was so happy to have him back. Because I had followed a trail of music to reach him, I felt inspired to write a song about my search for him. The words to the song go like this:

Kupuna Ei Nei   **Grandfather Ei Nei**
'Auhea wale 'oe? 'Auhea wale 'oe?
  Where are you? Where are you?
Pua makamae, E Kupuna Ei Nei
  Never fading flower of my *Tūtū*, Sweetheart
E lohe 'o wau 'o 'oe, i luna o Kona
  I heard you were in Kona
Hau kau i nihi hele, loa i ke ala
  Following a long zigzag journey down the road
E lohe 'o wau 'o 'oe, i luna o Waipi'o
  I heard you were in Waipi'o

Aia naʻe kalo, kaumaha nō!
> But the taro was too heavy!

E lohe ʻo wau ʻo ʻoe, i luna o Puna
> I heard you were in Puna

Ua naʻe mīkana, kiʻkiʻe no
> But the papaya was too tall

Eia ala ʻoe, ʻowau i hope loa
> There you are, I finally found you

Hānai a hulu, iʻa o Waipuna
> Caring for the fish of Waipuna

Haʻina ia mai ana ka puana
> Let the echo be heard

Pua makamae, e Kupuna Ei Nei
> The precious flower of my Kupuna,
Ei Nei

A few years later, when we moved to Kona, Grampa Tommy stayed in Hilo. He's in his 80's now. If you happen to be in Hilo on a Thursday at around noon, you may still see him walking along Ponahawai Street, a small man, posture still erect, hands clasped behind his back, head bowed, on his way to play music in his special style at the Salvation Army.

George Kahumoku's Selected Discography

Recordings:
- *Hawaiian Love Songs* (Dancing Cat Records, 2000)
- *Hawaiian Classics* (Aire Records, 2000)
- *Hawaiian Slack Key Christmas* (Dancing Cat Records, 2000)
- *Hymns of Hawai'i* (Aire Records, 1999) – Na Hoku Hanohano Award for Best Religious Album of the Year.
- *Drenched by Music* (Dancing Cat Records, 1997)
- *Ho'oilina – The Legacy* (Kealia Farms Record Company, 1995)
- *E Lili'u* (Kealia Farms Record Company, 1995)

With the Kahumoku Brothers:
- *Sweet and Sassy* (Kahumoku Brothers)
- *More Than Words Can Say* (Kahumoku Brothers)
- *Kai Malino* (The Peaceful Sea) – (Hula Records)

With Aunty Edith Kanaka'ole and the group Na 'Oiwi:
- *Hi'ipoi i Ka 'Āina Aloha* (Cherish the Beloved Land) – (Hula Records, 1979) – Na Hoku Hanohano Award for Best Traditional Album of the Year.

Compilations:
- *Kī Hōʻalu Christmas* (Dancing Cat Records, 1996) – various artists, contains one song by George, Little Drummer Boy. Na Hoku Hanohano Award for Best Christmas Album of the Year.
- *National Park Series' Sounds of Hawaiʻi* (Orangetree Productions) – various artists, features George's performance of *Mele O Koholā* (Song of the Whales)

Film Soundtracks:
- *Onipaʻa – a David Kalama,* 1996 Mele Anna Meyer film of the 1993 documentary reenactment of the overthrow of Queen Liliʻuokalani. Funded by the Office of Hawaiian Affairs (OHA).
- *Kī Hōʻalu – That's Slack Key Guitar* (Studio on the Mountain, 1992) – documentary features performances by Ray & Elodia Kane, Sonny Chillingworth, Leonard Kwan, Ledward Kaapana, George Kuo, George Kahumoku, Jr. & Diana Aki, Haunani Apoliona, and others.
- *The Hawaiian Way* (Hawaiʻi Sons VHS, 1993) – documentary features slack key guitarists Ledward Kaapana, George Kuo, Ray Kane, George Kahumoku, Jr., Moses Kahumoku, Eddie Kamae and the Sons of Hawaiʻi, Manu Kahaialiʻi, Malaki Kanahele, and vintage footage of Gabby Pahinui and Fred Punahoa.
- *Troubled Paradise* (Flying Fish Records, 1990) – various artists, soundtrack to the documentary film features five songs performed by George Kahumoku, Jr.: Kealia, *Hoʻoipo Kamahaʻo, Kai Malino*, Kona Inn, and *Na ʻOno O Ka ʻĀina*.